North Node Astrology

Rediscovering Your Life Direction and Soul Purpose

Elizabeth Spring M.A.

ISBN 1-4392-2689-X
ISBN 13 978-1439226896

To order additional copies, please contact us.
Archaeon Press
www.elizabethspring.com
1-401-294-5863
elizabethspring@aol.com

Dedication

This book is dedicated
First and foremost
To you, dear Reader
For taking the time to read it-

And to all my teachers
And loved ones-
Especially Harry
Sarah, Shane, Greta
Mildred and Wesley.

May you all be blessed;
And may we each find that
treasure
Which arises from love
Of self to love of Self.

ৡৣ

"Tis the good reader that makes
the good book; in every book he
finds passages which seem to be
confidences or asides hidden
from all else and unmistakably
meant for his ear; the profit of books
is according to the sensibility
of the reader;
the profoundest thought or passion
sleeps as in a mine, until it is
discovered by an equal mind
and heart."
Ralph Waldo. Emerson

Table of Contents

Introduction

"Purpose is the place where your deep gladness meets the world's needs."
Frederick Buechner

Writing a book about how to find one's life direction and soul purpose might sound a little arrogant or naïve, depending on whether or not you believe astrology has anything truly worthwhile to say at all. One's *life direction* seems to evolve through the mysterious equation of "fate plus character equals destiny." I'm intrigued by how that middle factor of *character* grows and is changed through our choices. How much free will do we really have? How random is fate? Metaphysical questions abound, yet I believe that it is in the making of character through our choices that makes all the difference, and the depth of the insight that accompanies it.

My hope is that this book gives you, dear reader, a rather "special and curious tool" to dig deeper into the whys and wherefores of character and destiny. Our life direction is like the arrow which we shoot through the skies, and *aimed or not aimed* it lands somewhere.

We choose our target based on what we know. And as for *soul purpose*, I share a common yet sacred bias here, in saying that it is ultimately bound up with our growing ability to love and be loved.

Similarly, as a counselor I'm inclined to say that one's life direction and soul purpose is about the movement towards healing and wholeness—for who among us is not wounded and less than whole? Our life direction seems to evolve as much by default as it does by purpose, and yet we sense that it's more than the "visible hat" we wear in the world. It is about our healing, wholeness and deep happiness, and this is different for each of us.

Can you remember when you first heard the words of the poet, William Wordsworth, when he said

> *"Our birth is but a sleep and a forgetting, the Soul that rises with us, our life's Star, hath had elsewhere its setting, and cometh from afar: not in entire forgetfulness, and not in utter nakedness, but trailing clouds of glory..."?*

Maybe it's true that life existed before this birth, perhaps not. However, embracing the theory of reincarnation is not necessary to get something out of this book—what I might see as the re-incarnational story, you the reader, might understand as the effect of early childhood experiences and parental DNA. Either theory works.

As you might rightly assume, my point of view is that I like the theory of reincarnation, because although not provable, it's a way to look at the world that holds the promise of fairness and justice. It's a hopeful bias—because we know that life is often not "fair" to a person in one life, yet it may prove to be somehow mysteriously "fair" over many lifetimes. The law of cause and effect, of *karma*, operates silently with its twin sisters, fate and destiny, in ways we don't fully understand from our perspective. Yet we may be able to discern an order and an invisible pattern when we look carefully—such as when we look closely at the tangled threads on the backside of a tapestry or when we see the "lay of the land" from the top of the mountain. The closer I look and the farther I look, the more interesting the patterns become.

What are these invisible patterns we might not see? A friend once said, "Be kinder than necessary because everyone we meet is fighting some kind of battle." What is that invisible battle we don't see in our friend? What are the invisible patterns in our life? What happens when we attempt to talk about theories such as astrology and reincarnation to non-believers? It is in these realms I seek to probe, and it is from that probing that the true story of "Cocktails and Karma" evolved.

So I accept reincarnation and astrology as a *"kind theory"* that challenges chaos and randomness. It gives me faith that there is "meaningfulness" to existence even if it can't be proven or discerned in one life. Without looking at things this way, life feels too cruel. Yet when we go to movies we can accept the drama and tragedy there. Do you remember being told as a child: "movies aren't real, don't cry"? What's real? Perhaps when we come to the end of our journey and pull the curtain back we may be surprised at who is the real "Wizard of Oz."

In the Eastern philosophy of Vedantic Hinduism we were all once part of the One that created this *great pattern* or Story. This theory of reincarnation postulates that we live through lifetime after lifetime of *lila and maya,* of play and illusion, till we arrive back at the place where we started at the beginning: as One. According to this philosophy all sentient beings are part of this evolutionary unfolding; each of us being like an actor in a role in which we continually "forget and remember" who we are and where we're going—all in a grand homecoming drama that we wrote and directed.

The legendary occultist, the "magus" Hermes

Trigmegestus once said: "As it is above, so it is below, as it is in the inner, so it is in the outer." Man is the microcosm, the universe the macrocosm, and in some metaphysical sense he postulated that they are One. He was one of the first to theorize on the synchronistic correlations and resonances between things. I like to entertain the possibility that these ideas may be true, since Vedanta Hinduism carries the weight of centuries of scholarly belief, and "old Hermes" himself knew a lot more than I do.

If you can suspend your skepticism about reincarnation and entertain the idea that astrological symbolism is a language best used to explore psychological and spiritual terrains—well then, I invite you to consider the theory that there may be something in your birth chart that speaks specifically of your life direction and soul purpose.

When you approach this material with an open and curious mind, then you come to the question— why do I have *this particular* astrological chart? Why was I born at this particular time and place? Did I come here to learn or experience something unique to me? This kind of thinking challenges you to question everything you think you know about yourself and to look beneath the obvious. This kind of thinking has led you to this book, and to the healing message of your North Node. It will take you to the ancient past life *parable* of your South Node as well.

Using your curious mind as a tool, you're ready to begin excavating the "soul's code" embedded in the ancient astrological points of the North and South Node, known in India as Rahu and Ketu. These nodes aren't planets, but *astronomical points* that have been overlooked in the recent past by astrologers preoccupied with *prediction*, rather than purpose. I believe they are true astrological gold.

Astrological gold? Yes, like the alchemist's *philosopher's stone*, these esoteric points in the birth chart give us a base to turn the Saturnian "lead" of mundane reality into philosophic gold. An astrologer might say they offer a mercurial secret knowledge.

A psychologist might say the Nodes intrigue a person *just enough* to begin the process of self-inquiry, and that it presents the psychological concept of "compensation" as being the essence of how the North Node operates. In the chapter on the North and South Nodes we'll look at the how the South Node holds the discarded parts of the self—our *shadow* qualities, and how the North Node seeks to bring wholeness to the psyche by *compensating* for whatever is not balanced within us. It holds our Soul aspirations and is like a guiding compass, or a North Star.

This process of looking to an oracle—or more accurately, looking for an oracular sign for direction, is like asking to make conscious what is unconscious. It's like unraveling a good mystery novel, and lends us a small but useful measure of control over our life. As Carl Jung once said, *"When an inner situation is not made conscious, it happens outside as fate."* How exciting it is to ponder the idea that we might have some say in our fate! Is it an interesting theory, or a gift of grace from the gods? You decide.

৵৵

Whether you are a therapist, astrologer, an evangelical or agnostic, this book is written you—for aren't we all hungry for spirit and thirsty for meaning? Who isn't looking for more to nourish a sense of hope and possibility? I love what happens when you compare and blend different attitudes—especially when you combine "Evolutionary Depth" Astrology with Jungian Psychology—it heats up! It provokes new ideas, questions and possibilities. One becomes challenged to see the similarities and differences and to speak across "party lines."

Here is where we each become students of the *Psyche*; here is where we each become a *contemporary alchemist* combining astrology and psychology in a crucible. And if you are willing to let go of your resistance to the mixing, distilling and re-marriage of these two, then you'll change yourself in the process. Alchemists know this to be true.

For a long time I considered myself a *Theosophist*, and I think I am still one at heart. Through that spiritual philosophy I learned that what was once hidden as esoteric teachings are now being revealed: truths don't need to be kept secret from the "masses and the uninitiated" any longer. Instead, Theosophists have taught that we've come into an age where we each communicate our truth—and no more "my way is the only way."

The author and Western sage, J. Krishnamurti, ushered in that idea at the turn of the last century, reminding us that Truth is a pathless land, unique to each of us. Now the great challenge is to know ourselves *just enough*, and to be healed in our hearts *just enough*—so that our deep gladness and the world's needs can meet, as in the quote at the beginning. In that, we find our life direction.

And so this book is written in that spirit—to share some distillation about life direction, relationships, and transitional life passages. I do not pretend to have all the answers, nor am I a model of how to do this great alchemy. I wrote *North Node Astrology* because I believe there is a *new way* to look at the blend of what the wise Swiss psychiatrist, Carl Jung taught, and what depth astrology can offer us. We can use

Nodal astrology for guidance, not just for prediction. We can use Jungian psychology to deepen and fertilize our vision and imagination.

The astrological Nodes are a magnet that pulls the astrological chart together, synthesizing and highlighting the confusing bits of paradoxical information in the birth chart. You do not need to be an astrologer or an analyst to understand any of this. You simply need to be willing to do a bit of self-reflecting along with your reading. I believe you may "connect a few previously unconnected dots" or entertain a few flights of fancy that will help you make decisions more in alignment with your soul's destiny and with the yearnings of your heart. Why not?

ঌ᎒

Carl Jung once said there are three key ingredients in *psychotherapy* (which means, in Greek, "attending to the Soul"): insight, courage, and enduring action. This book is about the first, because in finding insightful knowledge we are well on our way to discovering our deepest sense of Self.

Self with a capital S? Yes. When Jung was growing up he made a distinction between a part of himself that he called his personality "No. 1" and another part of himself he called personality "No. 2." He, and many astrologers and theologians since him, have talked about Soul and Spirit as being two separate but related concepts. In a similar fashion, I've chosen in this book to use <u>Self</u> with a *capital S* to designate that "wiser sense of Soul" and <u>self</u> with a *small s* to designate the more egoic personality. One could also say that it is from the healing of our wounded *self* that we find our way to know our wiser Self—this "Self" that unites our personal sense of self to the cosmic Spirit.

☞☜

Oscar Wilde once said: "To love oneself is the beginning of a lifelong romance." Isn't that a delicious and outrageous thought? Who doesn't want to rediscover themselves and fall in self-love again; to "re-invent" our lives and feel that sense of *Self*? Or maybe we are more humble and simply want to have "a more determining say" in our destiny and fate; and perhaps like a good makeover, we confess it's an intriguing idea. So one of the things we'll do is to play with the equation: fate + character = destiny.

Most of us believe, like Mother Teresa said: "We can't all do great things, but we can do small things in great ways." It's not always about what we do in life that truly matters, but *how we do* what we do. And how we *speak about* what we do—for example, I could say this book is about my re-enchantment with life and "my inner Jung; my inner wise man/woman" or I can say it's about astrology and Jungian thought.

So "life purpose" isn't about quitting your day job and moving to India to work in an orphanage, although that might be perfect for some. Life purpose evolves as we find meaning in whatever we do, and we do this by bringing to consciousness what we have kept in the unconscious; in our "shadow". This term *shadow* is about all those very human things we disown about ourselves—things we tend to not see or that we dislike, and all those things we tend to "project" upon others who either irritate us. Yet this shadow also holds the *"gold"*—those noble tendencies and talented parts of ourselves that we have been too blind to see. In astrology, we find this by inquiring into the Nodes—

These Nodes hold the leaden, stuck places within our psyches as well as the places of aspiration, dreams, and unsuspected talents. It takes courage and a bit of "reading between the lines" to get it. I remember when first reading the philosopher, J. Krishnamurti— I would have to frequently pause between the lines to see if I could catch the gist of what he was trying to put words to—it wasn't easy. The Nodal descriptions here in this book aren't dense reading at all, conversely, they are almost too simple. You still have to read between the lines.

It is humbling work to look at our South Node—to look into our past life story and this *shadow*. It is not for the faint of heart or for those who want to see themselves righteously or piously. Looking at one's "unfinished business" is a humbling experience, and daring to act on the suggestion of the North Node isn't comfortable at first. It usually feels unfamiliar as well. Yet it is through this integrating process that we glimpse the possibilities of a fuller life.

And as Jung said, the third part of "attending to the Soul" is about *enduring action*: the willingness to withstand the tension of the opposites—the tension of holding the opposing voices in our heads, and not to break the alchemical vessel with lack of attention or self-sabotage. We need to hold ourselves gently, so that we may transmute the lead, the wounded parts of the ego, into the gold of insight and action.

ॐ∽

Relationships are the crucible in which we become who we truly are. And not just romantic relationships, but also our relationship with Self, with Others, and our Work. Some of us whine about the hopeless "Search for the Magical Other," but beneath the cynicism I hear a yearning for something else.

The youthful illusion of being saved by "the Romantic Other" gets reinvented as we get older as we see how much we've used *relationship as an escape* from our personal journey or as a distraction or even a sabotaging of our own calling! The romantic fantasy has carried so much on its shoulders—it's carried so many of our hopes for deep soul connection and joy. It simply is *too much* to ask of any one person's human shoulders to hold so much of what is truly only ours to carry.

Our life direction and Soul purpose is a quest—a question that a workout in the gym, a pay check, or an internet search isn't going to answer. Yes, we're *googling* for new solutions to old problems, exploring new paradigms, but I think we're still going to have to pull back on some of our expectations, and be very patient with ourselves. As we live into the answers to some of these questions, we may find that even imperfect maps can be helpful.

ॐ ॐ

So, how we talk about Soul matters. Soul can be understood as an illusive inner sense of Self—a kind of personal embodiment of Spirit. We don't need to define it here, but rather to feel it. We could say that it's *an energy* that wants something from us; something that impels us to live up to whatever our full potential could be. But no matter how we choose to define it for ourselves, it is how we feel about our connection or disconnection to Self that either feeds or depletes us.

How we find our life direction is also crucial. We can fishtail around in the world of jobs, careers, vocations, and relationships but unless the heart is moved and old painful habits are released, we may stay stuck. When we make life decisions from an insightful heart-space we tap into the collective unconscious, which holds deep wellsprings of wisdom...pockets of gold as well as illusive shadow dragons.

Then what ails us? Is it our tiredness or aching back, or the fear that if we look deep there may be nothing there? My sense is that we are ailed by that fear—that sense of existential anxiety that there isn't any more to life, and even if there is we can't get there from here. That we're too old, too fat, too uneducated, or too lazy.

Or even worse is the fear that if we had our freedom to be all we could be, we could end up having to fundamentally change. We might have to go it alone, take a journey, learn new computer skills, or confront our "hardening of the attitudes." We might have to reconsider our attitude towards our friends or partners. Yes, we may say we want a fuller life, but we usually want it on our conditions. This is a part of that anxiety and "fear and trembling" the existentialist philosophers wrote about—the price of living an authentic life.

We often calm this anxiety by distraction and amusement rather than delving into the depths. We forget how anxiety and excitement are two sides of the same coin, as well as depression and boredom. Who can hold the tension of these opposites easily? Why who knows, you could annoy your friends if you talked astrology and offended their academic or religious philosophy. We keep so many good discussions going in our heads, and instead read books like this in bed before falling asleep.

But before you fall asleep now, I'd like to offer you a thought—if you choose to explore the mystery of the Nodes contained in the *mandala of your birth chart* I promise you that you'll find meaning there that incites a kind of "make-over" that comes with renewed self-confidence. Sales pitch? Yes...and I'll add that at the very least, you will find it interesting enough to be disturbing.

Looking at life symbolically invites magic and synchronicity, disturbs the status quo, and renews a sense of faith and trust. Why? Because when you see how your personal life story synchronizes with patterns that are larger and bigger than you, you'll touch on your connectedness with the whole of life. You'll get a sense that your life might have a meaningful pattern that underlies the apparent chaos. Now don't you think the unfolding story of your life—your personal mythology—deserves at least as much time as you give to caring for your body, your relationships, or your finances?

࿐

Although I've studied astrology since 1969 it wasn't until about 15 years ago that I became fascinated with the North and South Nodes in the birth chart. Before then, I didn't know there was a particular point in the birth chart that would reveal clues to life direction or our soul purpose. In fact, most astrologers overlooked at the Nodes back then, in their search for prediction, and it wasn't until relatively recently that the Nodes became one of the most talked about aspects in astrology.

The internet is a rich resource of sites where astrologers and non-astrologers debate the meanings of these astrological enigmas. (Currently my North-NodeAstrology blog site receives about 300 hits a day from curious people.) And the insight I've gained from studying the North and South Nodes has made an enormous difference in my life by reminding me of core beliefs I've held that keep me "out of alignment", disembodied, and not authentically me.

These North/South Node default patterns show me what ails me, but also what cures me. The clue is in the North Node. Each one of us is a wounded healer, a "Chiron" that knows best the medicine that cures. I call that medicine the North Node.

⊱⊰

Again, how we talk about Soul matters. This book isn't meant to prove astrology or to be simply a Nodal cookbook for the psyche, but rather to provide you with a soulful language to talk about things that matter—like purpose, direction, destiny and fate, without a religious agenda. You may find that the Nodes *points a way* like a Zen master pointing a finger at the moon. I believe it's through music, poetry, stories, and the symbolic use of language that we slip beneath the surface of the mundane to that wordless place where we feel inspired, and where our souls feel nourished. And so, along with the charted descriptions of your Nodal journey, I've chosen to interweave some of my own stories as well, so as to show how the symbolism and the particulars of a life can fit together.

⊱⊰

Have you found the place where your "deep gladness meets the needs of the world" as Frederick Buechner wrote in the opening quote? We often judge our lives by our work and our relationships because this is the alchemical crucible where our life story gets "cooked." But there's another way to look at our lives that doesn't just chalk things up to status, money, or marriage—or good or bad karma in this life or another. It's about asking questions such as: Is what I'm doing now in alignment with my Soul's journey? Is there a way I can know more about that? Am I using all the "unrecognized" talents I was born with?

Whether you have a job, a career, or a "vocation" doesn't matter as much as how you feel about what you're doing. Maybe you wanted to be a nurse, and became a nurse's assistant instead. The life direction and soul purpose might still be fulfilled either way, and hopefully this book will help deepen your understanding about whatever it is you do. I also hope it helps awaken you to consider new possibilities, as well as providing a map of the twists and turns in the road—those life passages that astrologers call transits.

Ancient astrologers pointed to the North Star. We know that a map of the heavens or earth is not the territory, but the North Node is a useful compass. And, the astrological road map that the planetary transits give us allows us to see the "transiting" waves of emotional highs and lows. Perhaps by using the map you won't hit the bumps so hard or feel it for so long. "This too will pass!" has soothed many a tired soul.

But still, you ask, do I need to understand astrology or even believe in astrology to use this book? No. I suggest you simply take this as a theory you test for yourself. What do you need in order to use this book? Two things: use your birth day and year to take a look at the chart (Look at the chart in the chapter: "Where's My North Node?") in order to find the sign of your North Node, and second, use a copy of your astrology chart if you want to delve deeper into understanding the meaning of the other planetary archetypes and transits.

You can get a free copy of your chart through my North Node blog at: http://NorthNodeAstrology.blogspot.com. So if you buy this book directly through me or the blog, I'll send you your "parchment birth chart" if you email me your birth information *including your birth time* if you have it. If you don't have your time of birth, I can still send you your *sunrise chart*, which shows your Nodes with all your planets, signs and aspects. The time of birth does not usually change the Nodes, nor the signs of the outer planets, which are what we are considering here. You can also get your birth chart on the internet by googling "free astrology charts." Because most of this book focuses on the Nodes and the life-changing transits that happen to everyone at roughly the same age, you'll only need to use your chart for a few sections of the book.

꙰

However, to get the most out of this book you will need a humble curiosity and an openness to consider a different way of thinking that goes beyond the purely rational. It's a theory—see if it works for you. Whether you are a Jungian analyst or a Baptist minister, a full-time mother or an older person reflecting on a life mostly lived, it doesn't matter. What matters is an attitude of openness to all the various ways we can say "Yes!" to life in all its mystery. So this book is dedicated to you, dear reader—may it help you on your journey.

- Elizabeth Spring January, 2009

Ways to Read This Book...

...how about from beginning to end? That is fine, unless you want to go right to the chapters on the Nodes. You'll soon see that this book could have been divided into two books—one, just on the Nodes, and one on the planets and their age-related passages called *transits*. It was a hard decision, but ultimately I chose to put it all in one book because each part is intricately bound together in a life. It's all food for your intuitive imagination.

It can be amusing to play with these ideas, but there's a serious side to this as well. The longing and yearning you feel when you're out of alignment with your Nodes makes all the life transits harder—so, the more resistance or reactivity you have to your Nodal life path, the tougher the transits will be. Although Buddhists remind us that suffering is an intrinsic part of life, authors such as Cheri Huber say that some suffering may be optional. Truth is often found in paradox.

A few readers may wish there was more Nodal emphasis in the first section of the book. However, the risk in doing that was to create "cook book style" writing that you, the reader, might not venture beyond. I didn't want to do that. The way it is now, you have a chance to read about the outer planets from Jupiter through Pluto, and also get a chance to ponder their effects on your life through their transits. Then you get to pull it all together through the sign and house position of your Nodes, their aspects and rulers, and ponder ways to prioritize and synthesize it all. I hope you find your own best way to roam through the kaleidoscope of this approach, and find the material digestible as well as provocative.

᚛ᚑᚌ

So, here's the menu: we start with Self and Story—because the sense of *Self* is forged in the crucible of *relationships* with family, with partners, and our body, I've chosen that as the logic of beginning with chapters on those first, and then moving to the *life passages/transits* we all experience at roughly the same ages, and then to what the *Nodes* have to say about life direction and soul purpose.

I feel that you'll find a more heartfelt narrative by reading this book that way, from beginning to end, and you'll see how thoughts build on each other and amplify—but it is still equally valid to start in with the chapters on the "*North and South Nodes: Your Soul Messengers.*"

However, a word of caution: If you read the Nodal descriptions without reading the introductory chapter on the *North and South Nodes first, as well as the North Node Compensatory Medicine* chapter, there will be a number of questions that are sure to come up for you. And, without reading the *"Going Deeper"* chapter to flesh out critical nuances of the karmic nodal story, I fear you may put down this book feeling unsatisfied.

One could also say that "Astrology; Myth, Magic and Mystery" is another introduction, or a prologue. It is in essence a copy of a talk I gave at Brown University and I'm including it here because it has some facts, twists and turns that aren't in the rest of the book. It explains a few of the nuts and bolts of this kind of astrology in a more direct way.

And for those of you who feel the lump of indigestion arising around the concepts of karma and reincarnation, I've included an important true story in *"Cocktails and Karma"* that may make the "chewing" on those ideas a little easier. I'm still not asking you to believe, but I am asking for *consideration*—a word whose origin comes from "with the stars." And for those who enjoy the challenge of making bridges with people who don't agree with you, then you might find some tasty offerings in *Cocktails and Karma* for heartfelt discussions.

કેન્જ

Astrology: Myth; Magic and Mystery

When someone asks what work I do, I always have to summon up a little extra courage before answering "I'm an astrologer." And the reaction is usually the same. "Really?" they say, and then after a pregnant pause and intense eye contact, they either quickly change the subject, or ask with raised eyebrows—"So how long have you been doing it?" When I say I started studying thirty-eight years ago, I often see a shy smile and hear their confession: "Well, I always wanted to try that, although I don't know if I believe."

That's my cue to say that I don't know if I actually "believe" either! I don't put much stock in newspaper or internet horoscopes, but I find them fascinating. I take them as a theory, and then look to see if my experience matches what they say. I'm actually quite a skeptical person, and I do know that I don't believe in any woo-woo *vibrations* from planets, and I don't care if Pluto has been demoted by the scientists, and I'm simply not interested in trying to prove astrology to anyone—but I am interested in explaining it.

And then I hear myself saying: Have you heard of the concept of synchronicity? Do you know about the Swiss psychiatrist, Carl Jung? Do you know about the Nodes? About then I know I'll need to have another cup of coffee because the conversation isn't going to end quickly. People are curious and they want to know more.

In 2003, according to the Harris Poll, 31% of Americans believed in astrology. That is roughly 100 million people; 1/3 of the almost 300 million people we are in this country. I don't know what the figures are now, but in this year alone, Americans will buy approximately 20 million books on astrology—which is 4 times the numbers of such books they bought two years ago. But still—it's the black sheep of the family in most circles. And that is because astrology, like religion, or alchemy or even the nature of love, is something that rational reasoning and scientific inquiry will never be able to prove.

I can easily accept the hypothesis that astrology, *may not be verifiably 'true' at all*, and that the planets in the heavens are simply the names we give to deep psycho-spiritual processes. But when astrology is dismissed glibly by people who have never experienced it, it's more than annoying.

So why does it work? It appears to be a richly symbolic language of the Soul that defies reason. And it works, as said before, not because of any *woo-woo vibrations* of the planets, but for two reasons. One, because when we ask questions in a spirit of sincerity I believe the Universe conspires to show us answers if we listen well. It follows Jesus' law: "Ask and ye shall receive."

The second reason is because of the grace-filled principal of *synchronicity*. The philosopher Plato, and the late Swiss psychiatrist, Carl Jung, developed this theory of synchronicity, which literally means "united time"—'syn' means 'to unite', and 'chronos' means 'of time'.

Synchronicity is the theory of *meaningful co-incidences in which there is no rational causal connection between event A and event B*. But instead there is a *meaningful* or *beautifully symbolic* relationship between the two disconnected events. Jung shared his discovery of synchronicity and his many experiences with it in his autobiography, *Memories, Dreams and Reflections*. His chapter on "Psychiatric Activities" was a particularly fascinating re-read for me, underlining the importance of feeling and inner awareness, coupled with the synchronistic phenomenon—as he says there: "Anything can be settled by an intellect that is not subject to the control of feeling—and yet the *intellectual* still suffers from a neurosis if feeling is undeveloped."

For me this also explains why there needs to be a feeling, a sincerity and something of importance that you are dealing with, in order for the "gods to intervene" in creating a synchronistic moment. Perhaps this is why when we use astrology or other forms of divination too lightly, the results are likewise "light." However when we come from a place of heartfelt emotion in therapy, romance, dreams, or prayer we may sometimes be quite shocked by what connections can be made. Synchronicity may take our conscious egos by surprise, but like a serious clue in a good mystery, it is something to be reckoned with.

In terms of astrology, Carl Jung noted that one's birth time and place is a true synchronistic event, and that astrology works because of it. (Ask any woman in labor how much *feeling* is in that moment!) Jung went on to say that "We are born at a given moment in a given place and like vintage years of wine we have the qualities of the year and of the season in which we are born." Jung didn't understand the mystery of this process, but found that by experience—that astrology simply works. So he used it in his analysis with clients, even though he was often reluctant to talk about it because he feared professional criticism.

But here's a good question—what about those twins or quadruplets all born at almost the same time, to the same parents, and in the same place? Since their charts will look so similar, what's the difference? The *difference* is that they each are separate and unique

Souls. The incoming story of each baby Soul here will look similar on paper, but we don't know how these Souls *lived out* their past life karmic stories. They probably had similar challenges, and perhaps wanted to re-incarnate with other Souls they've known before, but the essence of it is that they are each *bringing in variations on a theme*, and in this life they're going to *play out variations on a theme*. Their Nodes will look similar—but their responses will be different.

ॐ⚬ॐ

Astrology is what I do—it's *my spiritual practice*, and I believe in it as one might believe in any religion—and mostly because it makes sense out of the injustices in the world when viewed in the karmic re-incarnational light of multiple lives. This kind of world view, this kind of evolutionary astrology, reminds me repeatedly that our Souls are on a journey Home, and that on this grand Quest we encounter quest-ions, and we have chances, over and over again to make things right for ourselves. Every life is a unique path to its own home. No right or wrong, no dogma or rigid expectations.

The type of astrology I practice has elements of Buddhism, Hinduism and the Judeo-Christian world-view in it. And yet it's not based on any of these—instead it draws out of them a non-judgmental compassionate view of life, and adds to them a belief in the plausibility of reincarnation and the soul's pre-existence. This belief system holds that there is an evolutionary process moving the Soul from separation from its Divine Nature towards re-connection with a benevolent Source. It suggests that we have so much free will that our Soul actually chooses the time and place to be born into so that it brings over both the gifts and challenges from previous lives.

So, how does it all work? When an astrologer draws up a birth chart based on that very important birth time and place, it will show tendencies, or probabilities, but it doesn't show destiny. We still have free will. Each choice and every attitude in life builds character, and character and fate are delightfully intertwined. Why is it delightful? Because most astrologers believe in that formula of fate plus character equals destiny, then we can consciously work on our character. Fate can throw us hard times, but we create our destiny by building our character in response to what life presents us with. We use our free will to continually make choices, and those choices are either conscious or unconscious, and are based on what we know at the time. I've always liked what Jung once said about this: "Free will is the ability to do gladly that which I must do."

For me, I sense a plan of divine justice here, and a cosmic pattern that affirms a meaningfulness, and a divine dance between the macrocosm and the microcosm; between God and man; between the heavens and the earth. Astrology accepts the ancient occult saying "as above, so below, as within, so without" and so it presumes a relationship between the planets above and the earth below; between the numinous "mind of god" and the individual psyche within.

When you look at your own chart, you'll see a psycho-spiritual description of yourself that transcends one life alone. Every planet in the chart is karmic. Karmic suggests habitual patterns, and reflects the usual way or style you have of doing things—and it may continue over many lives. Some of your old habits serve you well; others seem to be trouble makers. So karmic patterns are reactive knee-jerk responses—they are your "default" patterns when you're not applying a lot of conscious willpower over a situation. Karma is not all bad, in fact, just like all the planets and the signs can be read in a positive and negative manner, your "karma" contains your gifts as well as your stubborn resistances. In a nutshell, karma is the law of cause and effect. But not all "karma" is obvious or linked in a fair and just manner *in this one life*, so the subject does get mysterious. But who doesn't love to attempt to understand a good mystery?

Character, choice, and fate intertwine in mysterious ways, and my focus here is not to predict, but to help you explore all the possibilities in your charts. For example, let's say you are born a female with blue eyes and red hair and perhaps an Irish background. It's also significant if your North Node or Sun in your birth chart is tightly aspecting Pluto. The closeness of your North Node to Pluto or the Sun to Pluto tells you that your father, and your paternal inheritance is very strong, and that you have a kind of intensity and charisma that other people may find intimidating at times. It also suggests that you may have lost a "gift" from the father—he may have been absent in some way.

This aspect suggests you are not going to shy away from the deep and sometimes taboo areas of life, but rather will be drawn to explore them in order to regain the gift. You will want to understand the challenges that your father and grand-father had, so that you can understand your family karmic inheritance and not act out urges unconsciously. There's a legacy with this aspect, and the goal is for compassionate understanding—and often forgiveness, so that you do not act out the karmic-genetic tendencies blindly.

Because the planets don't cause anything to happen, but merely reflect the climate of a particular time, we have free will in determining how we will play out the symbolism of our birth chart and the astrological weather of the transits. You can choose to play out your "karma" on what might be called a *higher octave* rather than a *lower octave*. The more you know, the more choices you have, the better your decisions—this is when knowledge becomes power. Wisdom and "character" is what happens along the way.

འ་ལྦ

Astrology works—and occasionally doesn't work—for many reasons. Like the Judeo-Christian concept of prayer, we ask and hope to receive. When astrologers, like other spiritual teachers or guides, move into the literal mode too much and attempt to predict the mind of God, we lose. When we honor the fact that spirituality echoes the mysteries of our lives, we find that astrological insight can be profound. It can inspire courage and faith in the process of life and death. It can give hope.

Magic and mystery arise when synchronicity is felt—when what you see in your chart and what you know of your life are congruent; synchronized, and reveal a pattern. Astrology is not meant to merely define, predict, or forecast—it's meant to stimulate our insight and make us whisper: "Ah-hah!" Its here to help us do what the oracle at Delphi commanded—"Know Thyself." It helps us make better choices, as it gives us a glimpse of who we are, where we've been, and where we're going.

⌘⌘

So here's briefly how it works—-by knowing the date, time, and place of a birth we can draw up a natal chart that shows the exact positions of the planets in the sky at the moment of birth. It's like a snapshot. And this snapshot looks like a mandala divided into 12 sections called houses, with planets, signs, and aspects. We know that every planet is a symbolic archetype with a rich mythology attached to it, and every sign describes a way of being in the world. The *planets* tell us who or what we're talking about—our Self, our persona/masks, our ways of relating—and the *sign,* such as Aries, Taurus, etc. describes the qualities of that planet. The *aspects*, like the squares and oppositions, describe how the planets, or the voices in your psyche, are all relating to each other. And it all describes something quite uniquely fascinating about us!

As we age and time progresses, the planets move, and so astrologers draw up a second *"transit chart"* that shows the current positions of the planets for any given moment of time—usually the present moment, and place this chart in a bi-wheel around the birth chart.

By doing this one can see, for example, how the planet Saturn in the sky, in its orbit around the Sun, shows up in both our birth and transit charts in a geometric relationship that can "predict" Saturnian times in our life. It remains essentially a mystery as to why this *correlation* between the outer movement of Saturn in the heavens *resonates* with the inner mystery of Saturn in our psyche, but that is the nature of **synchronicity**.

So by measuring the degrees of the angles between the position of the birth planets and the moving transiting planets, one can describe the kind of interaction, or the psychological climate of a particular period of time. Computers do this calculating for us today, and these geometric angles created by the second chart let us know how the planets are now interacting with each other. Are they in a tense and challenging square now? That suggests a tension between those two energies represented by the planets squared. If they're in a trine/triangular relationship they are supporting and enhancing each other instead. Astrology books cover all these nuts and bolts of astrology in great detail, so I've only touched lightly on these basics.

ॐॐ

What I am going to do instead, is to suggest that you go right to the heart of the matter. And that heart is embedded in the essence of your chart: in the *North and South Node axis.* Think for a minute of the image of the medieval navigation device, the astrolabe—it's a double circular globe with an arrow shooting through it. The arrow is like the Nodal axis, pointing through to what I call our personal North Star, our North Node. This arrow unifies all the details of the complex chart—saying "Look here—this is where you are meant to go. This is direction of the North Node."

So how can you understand these most ancient, yet new, aspects in *your* chart? As an evolutionary based astrologer I see value in delving into the theory of the past life "parable" as it shows up in the South Node and how it affects the present life. This past life pattern that emerges through the South Node of the Moon may not be literally true, but I believe it holds "emotional truth." Like in a good story, when something reaches deep into the heart and resonates—we know something is hitting home. Literalism in facts is not what is being looked for here.

The emotions that are so often locked up in us could be the result of early childhood development, or the residual result of karmic dramas of past lives. They could feel, in moments of reverie, like a barely conscious memory of a dream. Or, like "incest that we barely remember" it may be an emotional truth if not a literal truth. The mood, like the Moon is still there, influencing the moment, but it may be obscured, in the dark.

This lunar "South Node hangover" influences our experiences in this life now. It acts as an invisible magnet beneath consciousness, and we are wise if we know our moods and tendencies to be pulled certain ways. We can act out the old story lines of default habits and past karma, or create a new story, based on fresh aspirations.

What's exciting for me in all this "theorizing" is that as we learn about our chart, the Nodes, and the transiting "weather forecast" the planets offer us, we get the chance to release these emotions locked up in past lives and heal them. We get to do something new as well. The North Node is very pragmatic in offering suggestions, compensations, and practical ideas. In the Nodal axis we see where we have repeated old themes and in the North Node we glimpse what we've often *denied* seeing about ourselves—and this includes forgotten and unused talents as well! The North Node and Jupiter "hold" not only suggestions, but hints of forgotten innate talents that we have yet to discover. And with these new ideas and insights we become freer to make better choices.

ح‌ه‌عہ

Astrology is a fascinating blend of myth, magic, and mystery. Ultimately, it can be a deeply compassionate tool that we can each use to help chart our course in life.

We understand astrology to be a soul language that confronts us with the puzzle that is us—we take it apart and put it back together in order to find the invisible connecting threads between what we know, and what we don't know.

Good astrology seeks to confirm, to comfort, and to subtly guide. A good astrologer is compassionate, hopeful and healing. In this book, you are the astrologer and the client. You are the mystery, and the problem to be explored.

Chapter 1.

"Cocktails and Karma: Reincarnation Anyone?"

"Let us give thanks for this work
That repeatedly shows us how wrong we may be—
That what we see first, is not all there is—
That people are far richer, more complex
And nobler than we imagine,
And that what we see as God or human flaw
Is flawless in design.
For the gift is in the effort—
In the practice of reaching to understand
All the unknowable mysteries
For which we are so truly grateful."
-Elizabeth Spring

I was at a party last Saturday night talking to a reformed-Baptist minister from rural Rhode Island. It was late enough in the evening so I was sufficiently soothed by food and drink to attempt a real conversation with someone on the other side of the philosophical waters. It's good to create bridges, I thought.

"The trouble," he said, "is with evil. People get shut down by the tragedies they see in the world—they don't see enough justice happening in their lives."

"Ah, you mean like 'When bad things happen to good people' I asked, wondering if he knew the book I was thinking of—the one written by the Rabbi scholar that had helped me when I was going through a difficult passage at my first Saturn return at age twenty-eight.

"Yes..." The minister had tired soft blue eyes. "I've been reading the new book *Why Good People Do Bad Things.*" He turned his intense gaze on me while biting into a chocolate éclair. "So how do you make things 'right' in your astrological world? Is it just that bad things happen 'under a bad moon'?"

"No, it's not so easy," I said, pouring myself a full glass of Pinot Noir. "Astrologers help people recognize life cycles and trust the process of change, especially when they're going through hard times. It's a bit like being a cosmic cheerleader." That's a truthful, but light-hearted reply I thought, as I was absorbing the fact that a minister was asking an astrologer a philosophic question. It seems that it's only rarely, at times like this—at the late night cocktail party—that "non-believers" are open to discussing a taboo subject like astrology. I remembered how Carl Jung was warned not to discuss alchemy or astrology lightly, as it might sully his reputation. I had nothing to lose.

As he stood there licking his fingers, it occurred to me what an opportunity this was to create a bridge between our worlds, yet I wondered if I would have the energy or tact to do it skillfully. I'm a Libra sun sign, and I must admit I prickled at the thought of real confrontation just now, but his kind eyes inspired me, so I went on: "Do you remember that religious question—-the equation that says: if God is all knowing, and if God is all powerful, then can it be true that God is all loving?"

I looked up at him and saw him suddenly raise his eyebrows. I couldn't tell if he was remembering that equation or getting ready for battle, so I quickly added: "It just doesn't equate for me that if God is all knowing and all powerful that he could allow evil to exist. It would be like a mother allowing her child to be hurt when she could do something to stop it....that is, if she was all knowing and all powerful." I could hear a pleading quality in my voice.

"I know," he said, "but because God loves us he's given us free will and in giving us the freedom to choose, then the possibility for evil enters in." He spoke as if he had said those words too many times before. Leaning over the wine table he perused the choices for a moment and picked up the bottle of sparkling water and poured himself a glass.

"Interesting conversation you two are having....!" A woman who I knew only as a local psychologist walked over and interrupted. "Have you ever heard of Matthew Fox?" she asked. The minister shook his head no. "He writes that we're meant to co-create with God by choosing goodness and creating new solutions to the problem of evil." Perhaps she was hoping that this famous Christian writer could be a bridge between us.

"Oh yes, now I remember." The minister seemed to light up for a moment. "He was the maverick Catholic monk who challenged the Pope! Yeah, everyone thinks they're right in some way. Each side in an argument or war believes they've got God on their side. Even astrologers too, eh?" He turned to me. "So, can you guess what sign I am?"

My heart dropped. "I don't do that kind of thing," I replied, as a wave of weariness crashed over me. I took a long sip of wine, and looked back at the minister, "But since you brought up the subject of evil, most astrologers think about that quite a bit. Many of us think that God's justice isn't often evident in one life, but it doesn't mean it doesn't exist. We think it takes *lifetimes* for divine justice to happen. It's a mystery—because we don't get to see the progress of a soul over so many lives. "

"God's got the mountaintop view, for sure, it's we who don't" he replied. "We just have to hold to our faith and not get discouraged. It's hard to feel powerless, to feel like you're strung on the cross, and to wait, to simply *wait*." He turned his gaze so intently at me for a moment that I wondered what he was waiting for, or expecting from me. Then he spotted another chocolate éclair next to us. He picked it up and smiled at me. "You look like you were born Irish Catholic, am I right?"

"Oh, yes." I could hear the ministerial voice advancing in my direction, and I literally stepped back. "A recovering Catholic," I laughed, but noticed I bowed my head.

"Nothing wrong with that," he said. "Always time to recover and time to be reborn....there's great peace in being able to surrender to divine will."

"Surrender?" I said too loud. Surrender is a hard word for a woman with an Aries Moon and Aries rising. "Surrender to a God who allows only one chance in one lifetime to get it right? What if you're born into abuse and poverty?" I could feel my steam rising. "Even a good mother gives her child a few chances to get something right. That's why I believe in reincarnation—we get many chances to get it right. Isn't it a little righteous for Christians to believe they can know from their interpretation of the Bible, who and what is right or wrong, or good and evil? It feels sort of righteous."

He didn't say a word but let my words echo around us. Did I really say that? My Libra Sun blushed, as my Aries Moon was rising up from slumber. Here was a challenge. I began pleading my case, waving my hand in the air like some Italian orator: "I trust, like you, that there is a benevolent order behind it all that we ultimately return to—but my "God" just doesn't look like your God. In fact, my God may even have a "shadow" unconscious part of himself." Did I just say "*himself*? "The only thing that makes sense to me is reincarnation and the pattern of cause and effect—you know, karma." I took a breath.

Any good Libra Sun would be heading for the hors d'oeuvres by now. Instead, I touched his arm. "Sorry, I didn't mean to get so wound up. Can I tell you a little story I just remembered? It's about good and bad luck, but you could also think of it as being about good and evil, or karma." He nodded ever so slightly, and so I began:

> *"Once upon a time a farmer had a horse. But one day, the horse ran away and so the farmer and his son had to plow their fields themselves. Their neighbors said, "Oh, what bad luck that your horse ran away!" But the farmer replied, "Bad luck, good luck, who knows?"*
>
> *The next week, the horse returned to the farm, bringing a herd of wild horses with him. "What wonderful luck!" cried the neighbors, but the farmer responded, "Good luck, bad luck, who knows?"*
>
> *Then, the farmer's son was thrown as he tried to ride one of the wild horses, and he broke his leg. "Ah, such bad luck," sympathized the neighbors. Once again,*

the farmer responded, "Bad luck, good luck, who knows?"

A short time later, the ruler of the country recruited all young men to join his army for battle. The son, with his broken leg, was left at home. "What good luck that your son was not forced into battle!" celebrated the neighbors. And the farmer remarked, "Good luck, bad luck, who knows?"

The minister looked like he was trying to digest that one. "I'd say that farmer was a wise man. He trusted in God—that is, he had faith that he couldn't really know what was good or bad."

I nodded my head in agreement. "So what we agree upon is that good or evil and lucky or unlucky is not always evident in the moment. You might call it surrender, I call it acceptance of a process...and astrology gives me a perspective about cycles of time so that I can see things from a more objective perspective."

The therapist nodded her head: "It reminds me that Shakespeare once said: 'Nothing's either good or bad, but thinking makes it so.'"

We all smiled knowingly. Then she went on: "However, the problem with astrologers like you, and Christians like you, is that you both make people feel guilty at themselves or mad with God, when things go wrong! You know, if I'm having a Saturn transit—to speak your language—it's still my fault!"

How impressive to combine Shakespeare, astrology, and Christianity into one swift verbal kick! At this point I was making quick guesses as to how Saturn might be making a harsh square to Mercury in her chart, when the minister came back with a quick defense.

"Oh no, it was the Puritans who believed that if you were a good religious person then only good things would happen to you, and that if you didn't live up to the word of God, then bad things would happen. Today we just say that we can't always understand God's will for us—but then, you're right—people do get mad at God for allowing evil or pain to come into their lives."

The psychologist shot me a look that could kill. "Yes, but then in the '70's you "New-Agers" started resurrecting that old Puritan idea that we are somehow all responsible for everything—by saying how we create our own reality. Remember? So if something bad happened, you'd say: so why did you do that to yourself? You know you're responsible on some level for your cancer...or whatever.... you shamed us again!"

Well, this was heating up in good Martian style, and the synapses in my brain started firing off: "No, there's a difference." I said. "First of all, you can't throw all new age philosophies into one soup and say that's astrology—even among ourselves we don't agree on everything."

"I know." The therapist smiled and took a sip of something that looked like Pinot Grigot in a long stemmed glass. "I have to confess, I've had my chart done! It's fascinating. The astrologer who did it had written a book about how the chart is like a blueprint or a time-line for events on a soul-level. And she said that it's the Soul that creates the reality, not the conscious person....she said the soul chooses to re-incarnate for purposes that our egos will never know."

"Wow! Well said!" I was impressed by this confession of her astrological explorations. I looked at the minister to see how he was swallowing that one.

"Well, reincarnation was accepted by the early Christians—but you're going a little far by saying an astrologer is going to know *why* the Soul reincarnates!" The minister started tapping my hand with his sticky fingers. "Ah, is it the truth vs. the Ouija board now? Astrology or God? Do you think you know the Soul's agenda, my dear? Maybe I should be taking notes for my sermon tomorrow?" He was laughing, but I wasn't going to let him sidetrack me. I pulled my hand back and pointed my index finger right at him.

"Look at it this way: *Who* is the one responsible? I see a conscious ego and a mysterious Soul. Two parts of us. One dies, and one lives on. We have an ego that we identify with—we call that our Sun sign, but aren't we more than this ego-centric self we've created? Aren't we more than this person who has a story full of drama, trauma, sin and glory?" We all laughed.

I noticed the therapist was wearing a professional pin of some kind on her lapel, and the minister had a cross in the same place on his suit. But where was my shield or button for my club? Get over it, I thought to myself, as I felt myself reach out to the wall for support.

The minister looked like he was choosing to space out for awhile, but the therapist held her ground: "Some astrologers think they can read all this in the chart, right? I know someone who says she can tell you about your past life. Do you believe that?" I heard the hint of disbelief in her voice. Astrologers must sound arrogant and righteous at times.

"Well, I would only go so far as to say the chart tells a parable of what our reincarnating story is about. It gives hints, not facts. Those are what the North and South Nodes in the chart give us clues about. But there are a lot of ways we can play out the stories of our lives, and I think it's dangerous to get too literal. But it can re-awaken the soul to a vague memory of what went before....." I noticed my wagging finger was now making circles in the direction of the minister.

"A vague memory? You mean the Soul has a memory, like a hangover from its past lives?" He took another sip of his sparkling water. He certainly wasn't going to have a hangover tomorrow. But I might. I poured myself another glass of Pinot Noir as the noise in the room seemed to get louder.

"Yes," I continued, "you could say that the rein-carnating Soul has an emotional memory of all its past lives, from the habits or karma it's acquired—that's called the South Node. But what's really interesting is that we also each have a guiding star, a North Node, that helps us chart our course in life. It's where our Soul yearns to go towards...." The minister looked like he was lost in a reverie for a moment, so I touched his sleeve to bring him back into the conversation. "Hey, are you still with us?"

"I'm here. I hear you, but what feels good or right for one person, doesn't always feel good or right for the other. Perhaps it's just a different language that's hard to get around—these Nodes and all this chart business, it sounds so mathematical and intellectual almost. " He ventured a kind smile, and I forgave him instantly. "My question to you, or anyone else would be this—how much have you learned to love?"

Zing! I could feel a shiver run up my spine. He got it, perhaps better than I did. I took a deep sigh. "That is the ultimate question, isn't it?"

"It is. But I can see your point too—if we under-stand ourselves and each other better, then it's easier to love. Without understanding, there's little hope for love."

"But I still don't get why a person, a soul, would *choose* to be born into an abusive family or get cancer at twenty-two!" the therapist added, looking a little snarly, but perhaps that was my projection. I bet her heart has been broken many times by some of the stories she heard.

I re-adjusted my voice into my wise woman persona: "I think that difficult lives are not punishments but opportunities for spiritual growth. And in some mysterious way it balances or repairs an injustice or ignorance...or heals a family. For example, an ambitious Soul in that space *between lives* might choose a short or difficult life. But it may have reasons we know nothing about. Maybe it wants to learn certain lessons for itself. Sometimes I wonder, why does anyone go to a scary movie, you know?" I could hear myself losing my wise woman persona now. I hate it when I hear myself saying "you know."

"Really?" She was listening beyond my persona. "So you're saying that the Soul, on some mysterious level, chooses to be born into a bad situation even though it could evolve into a victim or criminal situation?"

"Yes. And it's only from this deepest level that we can say we're responsible for things that happen to us." I remembered the metaphysical writer, Ken Wilbur, writing about this confusion of levels across the metaphysical playing fields, but there was no way I could retrieve the details of that information at this time of night. But a distant memory surfaced: "I remember an older woman, a Theosophist, once telling me that there's also a family and a national karma as well as personal karma, and that karma is not a tit–for-tat kind of thing."

She let out a deep sigh. "I don't know. Your words sound good, but I hear this undercurrent of making the victim responsible for something awful that is happening to them. That doesn't feel right."

I must admit I agreed too, and the minister nodded his head. "If we have free will you've got to admit there's some level of responsibility...at times. But in the struggle between good and evil, we can't control or even know what God's will is for us."

"Astrologers try." I grinned mischievously. "Sometimes I think we attempt to read the mind of God."

The therapist got hooked on that one, and rose to the occasion. "God's mind! God's will! I can get *really angry* at God when something bad happens to someone I love."

She was now pointing an accusatory finger at me; I flinched and cut her off—"But what if—what if on some mysterious level you made a **contract** before birth to choose a challenging life? Then couldn't you accept the idea that what *looks* totally irrational might not be? And just what if God or some benevolent power gave us a chart, a life map, that we could use to understand things better? Could you accept bad things happening to good people then without getting so mad—if you saw things in terms of evolution and cycles of life?" She was still frowning.

"We call that life map the Bible." The minister raised his eyebrows and went on teasing: "Maybe you two have issues with anger at God?"

I wondered if maybe I did. And maybe I really was angry with the attitudes of some ministers and therapists, but not with the two people in front of me now. I was thoroughly enjoying the verbal debate. "Oh yeah, I do. And maybe we make a mistake when we use words like good and bad because from the soul's perspective, who knows?" No comment. I couldn't tell if they were looking tired or just thinking about that one. But I wondered if the moment of bridge-making was beginning to collapse.

Yet I strode on: "I'd rather be angry at my own choices rather than feel angry at God or at a random, chaotic universe. But you know," I said as I leaned closer to them, "in this way of thinking, the soul really has a lot of free will. It makes choices as to where and when to be born...and to whom. And then it forgets it all."

The minister's bushy eyebrows rose again. "Forgets?"

"Yes, it forgets," I replied, thinking that there was just one more thing I could say that maybe they could hear. "Did you ever hear the old Hassidic myth about forgetting? I'm sure you remember that reincarnation was once part of the Judeo-Christian tradition, and that wise men once looked to the stars..... but anyway, there's an old Hebrew story about how an angel comes to each baby just before it's birth and as she blesses the infant she places her index finger on this little indented spot right here above the lips and below the nose, and impresses her finger there, telling the Soul to forget everything that has gone before the moment of birth."

"That's a sweet story," he sighed. "So perhaps we can trust in the angels as well as God, and not be angry then."

"Or discouraged," the therapist added.

I began thinking how hard her job must be. I wondered what she really believed in that helped her trust her trust the process of life, and to put evil into a larger perspective.

She took off her glasses just then and looked like a lawyer making her closing statements: "I don't think you can prove any of this. It still feels too much like blaming the victim, and it's all too sad. Too intellectual, for me, I stay with the body's truth. But it's good for you both to try to bring as much hope into the world as you can." She smiled weakly as I noticed her glassy watery eyes. I couldn't help but wonder how much pain she had suffered in her life and in her body.

"Maybe someday we'll all really understand what Jesus talked about," the minister added touching her hand lightly, "And then like that rebel priest you mentioned before, we'll each be courageous enough to tell our stories, and speak our truth."

The therapist started rubbing her tired eyes. "Or we can question our most basic assumptions."

"That's true," I concluded. I liked the direction we had turned. "And we can continue to build bridges between each other." I paused. "You know, astrologers don't think about everything the same way either, but we all think about life symbolically. You know: good luck, bad luck, who knows?" They smiled, and I thought—there I go again: "you know, you know, who knows?" My vocabulary was deteriorating, and as I looked with affection at my two new acquaintances, I also looked at my watch. It was indeed time to go.

I could see that we had come full circle and had each said and done just enough. We knew we could have gone on and on, but instead we simply chose to say good-night to each other, kissed each other on the cheek, and walked away to our respective corners and went home...each of us happy and 'right' in our own way. What a good evening this had been.

Chapter 2.
The Family Karmic Inheritance

"If we could read the secret history of our enemies, we would find in each man's life a sorrow and a suffering enough to disarm all hostility."—Henry Wadsworth Longfellow

As an astrologer I am continually struck by the potential for sorrow and suffering when first reviewing a client's chart. However upon meeting them, I am usually astounded at how uniquely they have coped, survived and even flourished in spite of the potential for anguish. How do they thrive in spite of their history? How do they forgive and let go of their past? Longfellow must have had a sense of it when he wrote that sentence, and if we change the word "enemies" in that quote to "families" then the most important point of this chapter would be made. If we could know each other's pain, this would indeed "disarm all hostility." I believe that the oracle that speaks through the language of astrology teaches compassion.

It has been said that the soul is ruthless in seeking its own path home, and that the needs of the soul, not the desires of the personality, orchestrate our lives. I have been finding that there is a mystery and history to each of us that reaches back beyond our present lives directly to our family lineage. We've inherited a karmic legacy that reflects the victories, defeats, and hard won battles of our ancestors, for they are indeed very much with us.

Within families there is a karmic inheritance that is handed down the family line along with the genetic blueprint. We inherit deeply entrenched emotional and mental perspectives, as well as unearned propensities such as musical and mathematical talents. Yet unfortunately, we know that alcoholism, depression, abuse and certain illnesses are also inherited. We gladly accept the unearned talents—such as Mozart-like propensities, but a negative family inheritance such as the Kennedy family "curse" is not pleasant to think about.

Even if we believe that our soul "picks" our family and our karmic inheritance so that we can inherit both the gifts and the challenges needed for our highest soul growth, it's still hard to understand. Essentially the soul's choice of when and where to incarnate is a mystery. Yet astrologers believe that the synchronistic moment of birth is the key element in the life story, because it gives us a genetic, or karmic blueprint of the soul; a map of the psyche. By looking at our family members charts, we can decipher emotional patterns that have been playing out for generations. All that we've learned so far about the Nodes and the planet Pluto, figures strongly in this tale.

These karmic patterns are not in themselves innate curses or blessings, for our will, intention, and grace are always operating. But anything can behave erratically if willfully suppressed for generations. Carl Jung wrote about the personal as well as the collective unconscious, saying that both talents and troubles are to be found in the subconscious. He didn't say how the unconscious works its way through the family lineage, but he did claim that there was gold in the "shadow" of the personal and collective unconscious. I believe that we can use the astrological technique of overlapping charts, called synastry, to help us see that gold in the family inheritance, as well as the imprint of family shame and secrets. We can become conscious of what has been hidden, and become freer by stepping out of the secret matrix of familial denial. We can then make choices to express and heal rather than to conceal. We can change the pattern for the next generation.

Everyone, not just astrologers and Jungians, are aware of the unconscious nature of family dynamics and what I call "the family karmic inheritance." Just as we might see that we've inherited our parents' tall bodies and long noses, we might also see a predisposition for sudden anger or alcoholism. We might notice too that the males in the family pride themselves, and judge others by physical prowess and athletic ability. But what happens when mental illness, greed, sexual confusion, or insatiable power and control dynamics are passed along? Isn't it then that we question ideas of fate and destiny, wondering if we were born trailing not only "clouds of glory" but "clouds of dust" as well?

Most astrologers accept the theory of reincarnation as the basis for this inheritance, whereas other people see it more as some mix of genetic and emotional DNA. Evolutionary astrologers find the theory of re-incarnation makes sense as it resonates with a sense of justice that moves beyond the karma of one life, as it echoes back to the idea that the "sins of the fathers shall be visited on the children for seven generations." It's a thought or theory that I never liked, but everything I knew about the Nodes seemed to fit in—-at least in theory.

Actually I didn't choose to delve into this karmic stew as much as it chose me. One Sunday morning many years ago, I awoke with a confusing depression that had been building for months. I knew my Uranus Opposition was almost exact, and that the time for something to "come to light" was upon me. I had moved across country, to California, and had made significant changes in my life. Yet I couldn't feel the joy or freedom that is the "gift of Uranus" despite my efforts. As was usual on Sunday morning, I called my mother, and had another depressing conversation with her. She was threatening suicide again if I didn't return East. Nothing had changed in that area of my life, even though I fought the co-dependency by moving thousands of miles away. It was a constant litany of shame and blame between us, with tears and heart wrenching reconciliations followed by more accusations of abandonment and blame. I was on the defense, and as usual, nothing I said assuaged my guilt, anger and grief.

But this morning, the grief overflowed into tears that didn't stop. I was paralyzed; I had no psychic energy left to move out of this mood. I glanced at my chart and saw the same line-up of planetary archetypes, the same old story. But next to my chart was a "mythic" Tarot deck I had just bought, written by one of my favorite astrologers, Liz Greene. Because astrology pulls its symbolism from myths, similar to Tarot, I had bought this as a tool to go deeper, and to amplify what I knew astrologically. Now here it was for me at my time of need. I needed an oracle, an insight, something that could bring new light to this unending situation. (It's always hard to be objective about one's own chart! Asking advice from other astrologers or using other similar symbolic systems can be of tremendous help when you are blocked.)

So that morning I took out the deck, pulled the Ten of Swords, and read the story about it. On a divinatory level it said that this card marks the ending of a difficult situation, and it went on to tell the story of Orestes and the curse of the House of Atreus. It is a dark tale full of conflict and bloodshed involving Athena, the three Furies, and Orestes. I remembered that Athena, as a goddess of justice, is often related to Libra, my Sun sign, and the Furies have to do with feminine fury and unrest.

I could feel a shift beginning to happen within me as I wrote down what I read: "A family curse such as Orestes has to bear is an image of inner conflicts passed down from one generation to another, where the grandparents and parents have been unable to face life's conflicts honestly and the children must inevitably suffer until insight is gained." It went on to say: "A deep seated and ancient problem is now forced to the surface and something must ultimately leave our lives...we can now move on not merely disillusioned, but freed of some deep canker which has its roots in a past older than ourselves, and which our own suffering has released and redeemed."

I then went to my computer and pulled up the charts of my grandmother, my mother, and myself— three women linked by genes and an obscure family history. I had often felt as if there was some secrecy in the family history, yet when I questioned my parents and grandparents they would speak only of their successes, or of the failings of others. The same old stories repeated; and I found that probing questions yielded little. But now I questioned the nature of this family karmic inheritance by looking at the interconnecting positions of the Nodes, the Sun, the Moon, Chiron and Pluto. What I saw in this synastry of charts was a pattern of connections that was enough to lift the morning's depressing fog. At least now I could see—and once seeing, I could make an attitude adjustment. I could feel a mood of compassion rising.

So I pulled up my chart and had another long look at it. I knew that Pluto in the horoscope is the "Lord of the Underworld" and reflects the Law of Nature for which the Greeks had so much fear and respect. And there it was, strong and highly visible in my chart. While thinking about the mythological curse that the Tarot hinted at, I rummaged through my astrology reference books and found that a family 'curse' involves some violation of natural law by earlier generations. I read that one can expect Pluto to be strong in the horoscope for anyone who has the need to make peace with an inheritance from the past.

What makes Pluto strong? It's strong when it is in hard aspects to the Sun or Moon or to the other personal planets, Venus and Mars—and when it's conjunct a Node. In these situations it suggests a karmic past life inheritance deep in the unconscious usually connected with the family line as well. When I first looked at my chart, I didn't seem to have Pluto aspected that way. I looked again—well, Pluto was the "ruling planet" of my Scorpio South Node—there it was! A powerful sign to bring to consciousness whatever was brought down the family line.

So here was the challenge. How was I to make peace with my Pluto ruled South Node? I pondered the charts: my grandmother, Elizabeth English, had a chart with a predominance of planets in the earth sign of Taurus and—Ah! There was the Pluto aspecting the Sun with a tight conjunction. I couldn't tell which house it was in because I only knew her birth day, and didn't know her time of birth. But I could see that the South Node was in Cancer (family enmeshment!) with a North Node in Capricorn. I knew that she was born in 1880, and that she had been a talented artist as a young woman, and after she married she had five children and never painted again. Her husband died in his late fifties at his Second Saturn Return, of alcoholism. With five planets in Taurus, there were issues around money, security, and self-confidence, and with Sun conjunct Pluto she would have experienced many symbolic—if not real—deaths and rebirths in her life. In fact, her mother and sister both died young from "heart problems" and when her favorite son succumbed to alcoholism as well, she retired to her room for the rest of her days. She struggled in her own way to move away from that enmeshed and culturally defined Cancer South Node, and towards her more ambitious Capricorn North Node; yet she remained a woman of her time. Her artistic freedom was severely curtailed by raising children, like most of the women of her generation. Yet I remember her speaking with an inner authority and independence, and she carried herself with a quiet dignity and a pride in her children. But I also remember an unexplained sadness she carried, and I was confused by her stubborn refusal to paint again, despite encouragement. She died at age 74 when I was eight.

It seemed as if my grandmother, Elizabeth, never felt the deep emotional serenity and financial security that is the touchstone for Taurus—-without which Taurus folks cannot release all their gifts. She was financially secure in her later life, but the mystery of her abandonment of her art was never told to me— however, her only remaining oil painting is a dark Rembrandt-like rendition of a *fortune teller* reading the tea leaves in a china cup to a well dressed lady at the turn of the century. The painting was done in 1903 when she was twenty-three years old, and now hangs in my astrology office. Some people see only its darkness and the sad look on the woman's face; I however find it delightfully fascinating that my grandmother's last painting, "The Fortune Teller" foreshadowed the astrological work that I, her grand-daughter would do.

When I overlaid my chart on hers, and saw that my North Node was conjunct her Taurus Sun—implying that there was something about who she essentially was (her Sun sign) that could be an inspiration or a suggestion for me, I took that to heart. At my Uranus Opposition at age 41, I took my grandmother's first name for my own, and am now known as "Elizabeth."

The story continues with my mother—when I looked at her chart and mine, I saw that her **South** Node, hinting of the past life story, was at the exact degree of my Libra Sun. I know that any planet aspecting another person's South Node is an indication that the two souls might have been in relationship before in another life. Ah—yes, our enmeshment and struggles in this life felt "larger than this life" and to see that we might have "danced together" in some way before was not really a surprise. In fact, it felt like a relief to see that our connections were part of a karmic dance that had its roots long ago in other lifetimes. I suspected then that all my work in therapy around us was more significant than I originally knew. Our charts were riddled with conjunctions and oppositions—just like us.

Then I noticed that her Capricorn Sun was within 2 degrees of <u>her</u> mother's Capricorn North Node. So if the North Node was a "good suggestion" for my grandmother, then something about her daughter's life could be an inspiration for her. And indeed, my mother was able to combine motherhood with her art, and she painted up until her death at the age of 88. She may have learned, by negative example, what not to do with her combination of art and motherhood.

I could see our wounds. There were painful issues around creativity, freedom, and ambivalent feelings about motherhood here, as well as enmeshment and co-dependence. I could see the connections though the wounded secret trail of Pluto's pride, shame, and insecurity. I couldn't know the secrets of my grandmother's family or the specifics of possible alcohol abuse that her son and husband suffered from, or the pain of the early deaths of her mother and sister—but what I could see was my grandmother's Sun touching Pluto and her Nodal conjunctions with my mother and me.

My mother's continuing demands for both independence and connection, reflected by her own North Node Aries/South Node Libra were a painful struggle that demanded too much of me, her only child. In today's psychological language she would be called a borderline personality. In part, she wanted me to "mother" her, something I could never do well enough. But by virtue of simply living a long life, fourteen years beyond my father's time, she did attain some of the independence of her North Node Aries.

In my life, I've struggled with independence, artistic creativity, motherhood and career, but my Nodal axis of NN Taurus, SN Scorpio still warns me not to expect or take what isn't mine. I must use my own resources, not another's, and stay clear of melodrama in all its guises. As a potter, astrologer, mother, daughter, wife...there have been many roles and side journeys. It hasn't been an easy road for me. I've struggled to bring as much consciousness to it as I can, gladly accepting the positive artistic inheritance and motherly nurturance that has been handed down the maternal family line along with the pain.

And finally, when I pulled up my daughter's chart, I saw more correspondences and overlapping. She is an Aries Sun, (embodying my mother's North Node), and her Venus is in the exact degree and sign as my mother's Venus. Yet her Nodal patterns seem to pick up more on the paternal family line, and we have an easy loving relationship. Something has been healed.

It is both fascinating and overwhelming to bring up family charts and to look at the connections between them—yet delving into this kind of astrological analysis, this "synastry," is best done with an astrologer/counselor who is familiar with the technique. But even a glance at the intertwining aspects tends to open understanding and empathy.

In all the charts within my family, the aspects between Pluto, the Nodes, and Venus hinted of an inherited struggle with artistic creativity and relationship. It all echoed back to Elizabeth English who fought with the competing demands of art and children, and seemed to lose. I would never know the secrets of her heart, or what pain she may have passed on to my mother, but my heart was beginning to open. Astrology was acting as a healer.

In a much more radical fashion, we can look at other charts, such as our country's royal family, the "presidential Kennedy's" and see their history of greatness and loss and wonder what legacy was handed down the family line. In 1969 when Senator Edward

Kennedy saw the collapse of his Presidential hopes after Chappaquiddick, it was said that he actually asked whether there was a "curse" on his family. And indeed, if one examines this family there are elements in the family story that suggest this possibility, though a thoughtful astrologer would never call it that.

Call it what you may, what happens with the challenges that are unconsciously inherited down the family line? Sometimes a bad seed develops, as rage and alcoholism can insidiously move down through the family genetics. Some children, such as serial killer Charles Bundy, showed signs of this at the age of three when he encircled his sister with knives as she slept, showing the peculiar signs of inherited rage. What's happening here?

At heart I believe we are up against a mystery, because in each life the soul has free will and can play out genetic or karmic tendencies so many ways. We may be able to see the footprints of something in a chart, but astrologer's move into shadowy hubris when they dare prescribe "how it will be." Free will and consciousness gives us a great chance to change patterns. We don't have to pass these secrets and silences down to our children. Instead the "buck can stop with us" as we heal the pain of our own legacy. We don't have to perpetrate silent crimes.

Instead we can look at the heart of astrology— the myths that the planets are named after, and we can find clues. And we can study the Nodes to see how Nodal aspects relate to each other—and to the Sun sign that each Soul has chosen to incarnate into as its "vehicle". There are also certain features which appear in every myth about a family curse, and it usually begins with an individual's abuse of a God-given talent or advantage. Something positive gets misused or distorted through arrogance and pride, what the Greeks call hubris. The abuse of creative potential, which is sometimes linked with a subtle or not so subtle abuse of children, is made worse by the denial and hubris carried on within members of the family. In generations past, we hid our shame within our families. Today we assume it's all out in the "open" because secrecy is the stuff of soap operas and reality shows and the evening news. But shame runs deep.

In mythology, we see that although each generation and each person could expiate the negative family inheritance, or "curse" by accepting a certain degree of limitation or humility in their life—-they often choose not to do this—and this refusal to make what is unconscious conscious, or to make the necessary sacrifices needed, can be seen as an act of putting personal desire or hubris before the needs of the soul. Yet the soul's needs are ruthless, and require a transformation of consciousness to change the family legacy.

Consistent unconsciousness and denial can behave like a curse. Because we have free will, our behavior can change fate, although old attitudes with very entrenched roots are harder to change. In the case of the Kennedy's, one could speculate that the arrogance, ambition, and possible abuses of "Papa" Joe Kennedy (including his choice to have a lobotomy done on his first daughter) exacerbated a karmic situation that had its roots in the history and sufferings of the Irish people. Perhaps it's a long shot to think that way; perhaps not. But if one looks at he collective struggle of Irish against English, Catholic against Protestant, and the tragedy of the famine which drove so many of our grandparents out of Ireland we can see how this could have fueled his ambition. He may have groomed his children for political power in order to redeem, in his mind, the shame and tragedies the Irish have had to endure in the last few centuries.

It was perhaps the obvious flaw in his daughter would have caused him great shame, and he took powerful action to correct it. Could this powerful man have set in motion a set of inherited attitudes that produced both great goodness and unforeseen tragedy? Was his ambition and the shocking deaths of his sons a necessary sacrifice for the greater good of our country and the Irish? Perhaps.

Were John Kennedy's (and Bill Clinton's) sexual transgressions an act of hubris? When John Kennedy Jr. died in his night flight through the fog, was he acting like the mythical Icarus when he dared to fly on a foggy night? There was a judgment he made that night that failed. Could he have avoided this by observing the limitations of flight or the cautionary limitations of the exact transiting Pluto square which he was in? An astrologer might have cautioned him from any daring acts, and called his attention to his North Node in Virgo, which demands attention to details, yet.... perhaps all this is just speculation and hypothesis, but this is what astrologers do.

The opportunity to heal the pride, shame, and painful family legacy is a challenge, and the opportunity to act out the unlived talents of our family legacy is a privilege. We do it by bringing the issues to consciousness. We do it not to blame, but to bring to light the repressed painful attitudes, and to bring compassion to our past. What a unique chance it is to redeem what was once lost through ignorance, lack of courage, arrogance, or willful unconsciousness! Especially at each major life passage, such as the Uranus Opposition and the Saturn Returns we get a chance again to ponder our karmic inheritance and to bring forth all that is longing to be expressed through us.

On that particular Sunday morning, during my Uranus Opposition at the age of forty-one, I began to look at my maternal inheritance differently. The painful legacy of expectations and attitudes that my mother inherited from her mother was not quite a "curse" although her desperate expectations sometimes felt that way. I could see again my inherited gifts: the artistic ability and a feisty blend of persistence and tenacity. But now I had a choice. I could see what I would accept in this inheritance and what I would attempt to heal or to reject.

That day, the simple act of seeing the reflection of pain and grace moving through the charts lifted my depressive fog. I could see that I was not alone in my struggle to free myself, but that these women had struggled too, in their time and in their unique way. The mythology behind the planetary configurations enlarged my sense of Self, and it was comforting to see how the orbs of my personal mythology touched the collective mythology. My unconscious wound was really no different than Orestes' wound or the Kennedy family's wound. Until that morning, I had been bound in my family's karmic web until I began to lovingly separate and untangle the knots. There was still mystery and secrecy, but I could now begin to choose what I wanted to inherit.

I had originally tried to ease the pain of my family inheritance by moving across the country—thousands of miles away from maternal intrusions. But this was not going to improve my difficult family inheritance. External solutions to internal problems are the line of least resistance. It took a lot of effort to move, but Uranus, unlike Saturn, is not about "efforting." Instead, Uranian grace and insight comes like a sudden storm—in its own time. When I consulted with "the gods" that morning, I felt a sense of awe and a lightening of my spirit. I didn't know any more of the family secrets, but I knew there was not only a "blood line" but a karmic bond made of similar patterns along this family line. I felt we were of "one skin." It was a compassionate epiphany, and it was then that I changed my first name from Janet to Elizabeth. It was then that my heart began to soften.

By looking at such family patterns one can almost hear the ancestor's whispering: "This was my hope and fear for me and my children; I tried to do my best." One gets a sense that the soul's choices (the Nodes) are not always those of the conscious ego. The connection between soul and ego always has this mystery, this uncharted territory, leaving room for free will. And misfortune and sorrow are often the soul's last resort in moving a person closer to the right path for them. And who is to say what is truly misfortune? The soul's path is not easy to describe, and rarely simple to resolve. But we try.-

Chapter 3.

"What's Venus Got to Do With It?" The Alchemy of Desire: Healing the Wounded Heart

"What happens when love ceases to be the endorphin-filled romance of wine-tinged illusions but rather the wrenching away of all our hopes and even our sense of reality? This is not a time for failure of imagination—now is when we need new definitions of love and life to carry us through to the safe ground of sanity. What could love feel like? What would contentment be like? Perhaps the challenge is to re-imagine the possible and to re-invent a life while not indulging in tight expectations. If we can wait and "cocoon" while holding the tension of the opposites of hope and despair in these times, then what Carl Jung called the 'reconciling third' may indeed appear."

"You seem to have led a charmed life," her words echoed uncomfortably in my ears. Yes, after twenty years of marriage all the visible markers of a charmed and successful life were in place: a healthy child, a thriving business, and a beautiful home. But something was wrong, and I knew that beneath the beautiful backdrop of my life was an inner hunger so strong it was boring a hole through my stomach. I had an ulcer, as well as a fiery nature that fueled my dreams. I was 46 years old.

It was clear that my partner and I were developing different interests, but wasn't that normal? Where once we had worked in tandem on so many projects, we now worked independently, and what fired me up, left him cold. Despite all my noble efforts to create 'the good life," a sadness seemed to be creeping in, showing me that the life that once seemed to be good enough for us, wasn't enough. In my husband's chart, I saw that transiting Saturn was conjuncting his Moon—a frequent "signature" for serious events, if not depression or exhaustion. A slow fear began to envelop me—whether I plunged into my work or deepened my friendships, or quietly grieved with my journal, there was no relief. There were no Excedrins for my heart.

Because I owned a metaphysical bookstore and have read many of the books on relationships, I expected myself to move quickly beyond this confusion. But this journey was moving in a manner and time far beyond my control. My mind obviously didn't know what was happening, so my body began speaking up; anxiety attacks arose within me with no known cause, and I would wake at four AM with bolts of electric energy running through me. For months my sleep was disturbed.

As my body chemistry began shifting, I took myself to a therapist—a man who loved the books in my shop and who had a gutsy acceptance of the dark side of life. Because I believe the spiritual and the emotional are so bound up with issues around forgiveness of our humanness, I chose a man who was familiar with this territory. I didn't want to do a spiritual bypass on anything—I wanted to question myself, my partner, my spirituality, my expectations, and...to fix it!

Instead, my therapist gave me a copy of a letter that Carl Jung wrote in Bollingen, Switzerland in August of 1945. Here it is:

"Dear Frau Frobe,
There can be no resolution, only patient endurance of the opposites which ultimately spring from your own nature. You yourself are a conflict that rages in itself and against itself, in order to melt its incompatible substances, the male and the female, in the fire of suffering, and thus create that fixed and unalterable form which is the goal of life. Everyone goes through

this mill, consciously or unconsciously, voluntarily or forcibly. We are crucified between the opposites and delivered up to the torture until the 'reconciling third' takes shape. Do not doubt the rightness of the two sides within you, and let whatever may happen, happen. The apparently unendurable conflict is proof of the rightness of your life. A life without inner contradiction is either only half a life or else a life in the Beyond, which is destined only for angels. But God loves human beings more than angels.
With kindest regards,
Yours sincerely,
C.G. Jung."

Reading that letter felt nurturing on a soul-level, but a harsh reminder that there was going to be no quick fix. In fact, the first issues to come up were not even about my marriage, but were around my inability to forgive a betrayal in friendship and the constant pain of dealing with the suffering of my aging mother. Week after week I turned my attention to the work I was doing with the therapist, and I began feeling loved, heard, understood. I became receptive to his wise words and to the process we were involved in—and I began seeing meaningful connections in my life. I learned how to hold and protect myself by aligning myself with a higher power, and soon felt "full" enough to forgive my friend, and to endure my mother's suffering and constant needs. As an only child, I had always suffered the responsibility of her life in a way that was without boundaries. Now I was learning what was mine to heal and what was not.

I also felt how the deep and intimate relationship with the therapist stood in sharp contrast to the lack of intimacy in my marriage. I began aching for that type of emotional presence that I had transferred onto my therapist. I tried to bridge the gap with my husband but it felt as if we had no common language and little energy for it—we felt powerless and without words together. He also wasn't feeling good; he looked exhausted from his own work. In his own way and without words, he was hurting deeply and grieving too.

I however, was not only in the process of self-discovery and healing, but of living an illusion of sorts: I had projected my soul, my "animus" (as the Jungians would say) onto my analyst and withdrew energy from my marriage. I turned to the therapy, to books, to God, to going back to school, to writing. My expectations of how it should all be were falling apart but I was going as fast as I could to hold onto something.

As time went on, and the dependency and transference of love to my therapist slowly began to release itself, I felt the growing pains of my neglected marriage. I was plain lonely, and couldn't deny that I was moving through hell, like Persephone, always struggling to get unstuck and up into the light again. But by then my partner had disassociated himself from my hell, my pain, and withdrew himself into his work. I felt that I was alone in holding all the darkness and pain of our life. I wrote poetry and yearned for a deeper love. As the denial of our failing marriage fell away, we tried in all the old ways to being responsible to our duties, and we tried couple's counseling, but it simply brought up more sadness.

Synchronistic events often mark transitions, and that winter the diamond literally fell out of my wedding ring and was lost. With a cold and poignant sweetness, my partner and I decided to try to give each other the only thing that was left: freedom.

Yet nothing changed our lives until my body demanded to be heard. Astrologers often say that when the heart is unhappy, the Moon—our emotional nature, shows how it feels through the body, somatically. I went for a mammogram and it came back undeniably questionable. It looked like cancer. After many x-rays, I was advised to go to a Boston specialty clinic and get the definitive results. There machines could tell in a day if I had cancer or not. My husband didn't offer to go with me that day; this "emergency" was seen as a part of my fearfulness, my dark drama, not his. A friend went with me that crucial day as I found out I was not a victim to cancer, but to a broken heart.

Someone once said to me a rather sexist comment about separations: women grieve, men leave. Perhaps it is the feminine in all of us that grieves, and the masculine part that takes action. That day, I clearly saw strains of a self-imposed victim-hood and chose to leave. The masculine part of me rose up in anger, in freedom, and in the middle of a raging snowstorm—I moved out. I found a new place to live that very day, and summoned up all the courage I could to face the inevitable void. The planet Uranus was opposing my natal Mars then, and I felt impatient, scared, peri-menopausal and impulsive.

It wasn't so bad at first. With a new apartment, my creative juices flowed into making a new nest for myself. My husband and I agreed to never talk badly about each other in front of our teen-age daughter, and we explained our separation to her in the most compassionate of ways. She in turn, was compassion-ate with us, and never took sides or complained.

We seemed blessed with no high drama, so I thought maybe we could all just get over this, let go for awhile, and get on with life. But all the beautiful and sweet moments of our marriage and family life kept creeping back into my psyche. The feminine grieving had a grip on me. I couldn't let go and I found myself crying at every turn.

I've heard it said that suffering is a hard kind of grace that teaches us compassion. For twenty years I'd worked on a dream that was now shattered and I expected myself to just get over it. My persona of self-sufficiency hid my aching desire to be held in sweet surrender in a lover's heart. I was just beginning a crash course in compassion—compassion for myself and for all others who have lived through great suffering. Is it trite to say I was finally getting in touch with my true feelings? That I was outraged, terribly sad, and pissed as hell that it might take a very long time before I could go for more than two hours—or two days without crying?

Dating seemed like the best cure—or was it revenge? And it did feel good to have those "highs" of being seen and heard and courted. Yet by the end of that summer I stopped my dating. And that's when he began his serious dating. At this point all I could do was grieve and rage at our loss.

It must have been toxic right down to my gut, for when my body acted up again, this time it was with a serious attack of appendicitis that put me in the hospital for over a week. (This was a transiting Uranus/Moon aspect indeed!) The toxicity had spread, and at one point I thought that death was not a totally unwelcome probability. My old therapist visited me daily. My husband, who was very busy with his new love at this time, went through the motions of getting me released from the hospital, but he wasn't willing to sit and be with me in my fragile state. Twenty years of marriage sat face to face with twenty days of his new love, and she won.

I remember the night before leaving the hospital—I raged at his coldness, wrote volumes in my journal, and thought: "I don't have to burn anymore—I can choose to let it go." Nearly exhausted, but fueled by my anger, I got out of my hospital bed, turned up the music on my radio, and began dancing like a naked solitary spirit; moving my body slowly and rhythmically, letting it all go once again. I was being released. Something new was being born in me at that moment. My natal Moon sign in Aries had suffered a serious blow; however the Aries archetype is known not only for anger but for the ability to survive.

The next day I felt a great sense of gratitude for simply being alive. I pondered my choices, and knowing that my Libra Sun sign was conjunct Neptune, I had to get over feeling the victim and feeling that someone had to rescue me. I knew I had to endure some suffering, but I also knew I didn't have to shame or blame or feel crazed. So when my "ex" came to release me from the hospital, I had journaled, danced, prayed, and burned through to the place in me which knew that we were each doing what was right for us now.

"Letting go" is what I do now, over and over again. I realize how hard it is for me to let go to all the ways of thinking that trick me into believing that I am separate from the rest of humanity and special in my suffering. It's always a good idea to look at the blind spot in our birth charts—to the sign and house where Neptune is—so that we see where we may feel especially confused, without boundaries and permeable to the moody states of illusion and disillusion. These are all Neptune's realm.

In my birth chart, Neptune is in the 7th house of marriage and one-on-one relationships, and it is here that I can fall into these illusory traps of self-deception, wavering judgment, and hopes for redemption. Yet it's here too that I feel spirit in my life, and sense a spiritual process that is greater than my small ego. In one-on-one relationships I find and lose myself over and over again. As a counselor or in therapy, in marriage, or with close friends, it's an intense "dance" for me.

Neptune is the planet of Spirit, and not an easy one to hold onto tangibly. In Vedantic Hinduism they teach a way through these Neptunian mirages: they say we need to find what is true, by finding what is not true—-they call it "neti-neti" meaning: "it's not this, not this." And in finding what is illusory, we can find what is true beyond the realms of illusion and duality.

Most spiritual traditions encourage us to accept the idea that we are held lovingly in the heart of God, and grounded in a Oneness into which we can let go. I've been looking at this—testing it almost, and there does seem to be elements of grace and synchronicity that move me along when I trust and let go. It's a good practice, this: "neti-neti." The poet, Wendell Berry, put it well: "Willing to die, you give up your will. Keep still until, moved by what moves all else, you move."

Poetry and prayer are also powerful messengers and healers. When I'm feeling vulnerable, and being the earnest striving person that I often am, then I tell God what I need—one form of prayer. But when I live from the part of me that trusts, then I listen and ask, rather than talk—another form of prayer. And I've been wondering lately: what is God asking me to see or let go of at this moment? At these times I often find or write a poem that speaks directly to my heart. There's often a question being asked or answered, and when I'm receptive, I get it.

Get what? The answer I get is to go on being a person worth loving, and to "cocoon." That is, to process what's happening by giving my self some simple time and space without expecting too much too soon.

And as I began doing this, I began to suspect that I'd been unconsciously orchestrating a release from this relationship that simply had run its course. Astrology reference books are always teaching this harsh sense of karmic responsibility when it comes to describing a difficult transit by saying: "This may happen to you....or you may find yourself creating the circumstances to bring this event about." And so we are constantly reminded to move from an attitude of victim-hood and blaming, to one in which we own our own power and accountability.

Cocooning has its own rewards—while my heart waits to know one special love again, there is still grace and synchronicity everywhere, and I strive to be busy with the work I feel called to do. Sometimes I doubt myself, but mostly I have faith. I believe now that as my heart was breaking, it was also breaking open and softening, rather than closing and hardening. I've been choosing to soften, and to honor the truth of my story. Despite the wounds I gave and received, I strive to look at this separation with spiritual eyes, sensing that there is a meaning and a blessing here.

Cocooning into a greater consciousness is the great work for me now; and it's a daily job that brings not joy, but contentment. And when I feel the little unexpected graces—that surprise call from an old friend perhaps—then I know that while my heart heals, I am being held, and I trust.

☙ ❧

That was what I wrote at the time of my separation. That was published in *Spirit of Change Magazine*, and four years later I wrote this for the same magazine:

"Twenty years married, four years divorced, and now we're six months into seriously dating—again. It's not an uncommon scenario, but it certainly is one that makes people smile when we tell them how our divorce didn't work out. Like a good ending to a movie, love survives. Some people can heal. We're hoping we can.

Many years ago when I wrote that story about the ending of our marriage it was my way of making sense of what didn't make sense—a good marriage that unraveled for no apparent reason. I thought it was a brave attempt to delve into the discrepancy between the overt and the covert facts. The shock of our mutual choice to separate had sent me into a state of withdrawal and grieving, which I called "cocooning," and simultaneously challenged me to be in the world in a new way—wounded but not whining. It took a consistent and at times faltering effort to do that, to not shame or blame him or myself. I can simply say now that we didn't know how to do it any better at the time.

The question has come around again, and the answer remains to be seen: do we know how to do it better at this point? Have we really grown in such a way that we can now re-marry? We're hoping the answer is yes, but we don't really know.

Our story is not an unfamiliar one, yet the reasons people reunite can be quite varied. Loneliness and dismay at the dating experience are obvious reasons, but that wasn't our primary experience. My husband had loved and lived with a woman for most of those four years, and although he was never engaged, they appeared to be blissfully happy. They bought a lovely country house together and moved out of state. I, too, made a valiant attempt at happiness, becoming engaged to a man after a two year courtship. But

I found myself missing my old love at the strangest times. I would be the last to think that I would be beset by heartache while vacationing in Italy on the shores of Lake Magiore with my new fiancée. But these moments did occur, and eventually I broke off my wedding engagement six weeks before the marriage. (I do regret having hurt my fiancée, and yet I could not seem to change the course of my destiny, although I tried.) So both of our new relationships were serious attempts to disengage from each other and they each failed. Why?

Perhaps before getting to why, I should explain "how" we got back together. After I broke up my engagement, I went away on vacation by myself, and in the process of slowing down and allowing myself to really feel and assess my life, I noted over breakfast one day that I seriously missed my ex-husband. So I wrote him a letter right then, telling him that there was a split in my life that I felt no other man could heal. I wrote that we felt like an unfinished story, and that the bittersweet weight of our mutual history was deeply with me. I felt that I had been tragically severed by our mutual decision to separate.

I waited, and we talked a bit, but it took six months before I got a serious reply from him. He found himself unexpectedly in tears one day while browsing through the Hallmark cards; the anniversary cards were too much for him to bear. He too felt that our story was unfinished. So he called for a date.

So was it nostalgia? Maybe, and forgive me if I sound too romantic, but we've come to believe that we never really stopped loving each other. Perhaps we simply weren't conscious enough to see that a mid-life crisis, a passing depression, or a growing apart, are events that can be part of a marriage and not a reason to end it. We needed a healing and a time apart, but we came dangerously close to losing each other altogether.

Why couldn't we commit ourselves to our other loves? Since I don't believe in accidents but do believe in choice, I suspect we needed to do exactly what we did. We needed to experience in our new relationships what was missing in our partner to see if that made a difference. And so we found partners who supplied qualities each of us lacked. He found an emotionally supportive, consistently cheerful woman who, yes, even looked like me, and who helped him feel safe enough to do some inner work and therapy. She was not as demanding as I had been. And I had found a man who liked to read, travel and talk intimately about everything. He said "yes" to many of my dreams and, although he looked nothing like my husband, I must admit he had some of the same traits. (Being an astrologer I once jokingly prayed to God to never send me another Virgo. Well, "he" was a double Virgo! Who knows best what we need?)

It is still a mystery—the way love is a mystery—yet it seems to be less the fault of the significant other and more about how we felt about ourselves and our marriage. Why did we come back together? I've often simply said that we were deeply rooted in our shared history and felt "at home in the same soil" and so the transplant, the divorce, simply didn't work. But perhaps we were still haunted by our original love and our vows to hang in there through thick and thin. Perhaps we had also learned to see love as being bigger than the times when it feels romantically good, or when it feels depressingly bad. We had both gone into therapy individually and perhaps now we were more able to take responsibility for our emotions. My husband also explains that therapy gave him a "language toolbox" that he could use with me so that we could speak the same language, and put words to feelings.

The negative patterns of our South Nodes had emerged under stress and exhaustion, and it took time, humility, and suffering for us to reach out to each other again—and to reach for the healing hints embedded in each of our North Nodes. We were so numbed by our suffering in the beginning that we couldn't see what was being asked of us, or how we could bring in those Nodal qualities that had a lot to do with both of our South Nodes being in the 8th house. Unconsciously we may have expected 8th house trauma and disappointment. We had not attained the self-confidence in ourselves that the North Node in the 2nd house bestows—we fell back on our default 8th house, and so we truly "died" before we were reborn. Eventually we found and embraced a new way of being together.

Last weekend I was at a craft festival helping my ex sell his pottery. As I was wrapping up a pot in a newspaper I spotted a recently published article on Ram Dass, the spiritual spokesperson for many baby boomers. Three years ago, just before the massive stroke that severely challenged his ability to speak, he was told by his editor that his new book (being published this month) was too glib and not visceral or deep enough. Today he sees his stroke as a "fierce grace" which allowed him to know and respect the extreme suffering and vulnerability that can come with age. People close to him noted that the stroke changed him, making him more humble and compassionate. The truth is that it nearly destroyed his faith.

As I read the article, the similarities between a near-death experience, such as a stroke, and the psychic earthquake of a divorce resonated in me. The shock to the system, the tearing away of illusions and vanity, and the vulnerability must be experienced to be known. At these times the soul's ruthless orchestration of destiny confronts us with uncomfortable questions. If God is compassionate and I've been "good," then how can this be happening to me? Who's wrong? Can I redefine what is a loving God or a loving mate? Are "they" giving us what we want or what we need?

When we are in the midst of illness or tragedy, we are motivated to redefine our relationship with a loving or not so loving God, whereas redefining human love in relationship is a conscious choice not everyone chooses to do. It feels easier to start over or drop out.

In his interview Ram Dass noted that in preparing for death one prepares for the deepest mystery of the universe—"You prepare so that you'll be open, curious, and not clinging to the past. You'll just be present, moment by moment." This may be the key. In loving and in dying the act of not resisting the present moment allows the soul to have its voice. It allows for the unexpected, for newness, for a chance to see things differently. In not resisting what is, an attitude of acceptance frees the energy that was previously bound by old expectations.

Some people say if a relationship didn't work before, it won't work now because people don't change that much. Astrology would agree and disagree—our birth charts stay the same throughout our lives reflecting a basic consistency, but the transits and progressions reflect our constantly changing selves, as the same issues come round and round again to be dealt with in new and unique ways, and with new chances to bring in the healing energies of the North Node.

⬳⬴

I believe we are constantly invited to change and to re-invent ourselves. When the shattering of romantic illusions and all the small betrayals stand face to face with every real hope for peace, healing, and forgiveness, the chance for change is seductive. When I consider that my ex-lover/ partner has heard the hard edges of arrogance and fear in my tone of voice and feels the uneasy questions within me and is still willing to love me again...well, that's something to consider. In Latin, "con" means "with," and "sider" means "from the stars." Perhaps forgiveness and re-enchantment is a gift of grace "from the stars." Yet I believe we have to do the work necessary to be open to that receptivity, and that doesn't come easy.

Last week I came upon a poem by Wendell Berry that moved me so much I inscribed it on a clay tablet and gave it to my new "old love". A sweet synchronicity seems to be echoing here:

"How joyful to be together, alone
as when we first were joined
in our little house by the stream
long ago, except that now we know
each other, as we did not then
and now instead of two stories fumbling
to meet, we belong to one story
that the two, joining, made. And now
we touch each other with the tenderness
of mortals, who know themselves;

how joyful to feel the heart quake
at the sight of you
old friend in the morning light,
beautiful in your night robe!"

ॐ ॐ

Healing the Wounded Heart; the Astrological Perspective

That was the end of the second article. Now we are eight years remarried. We still struggle with all of the same issues—but incrementally we're bringing more love and understanding into accepting the ways we're different and the ways we're the same. We are an example of a classic marital problem: I have a fear of abandonment, he has a fear of engulfment. We both share the same values, and desire for intimacy and connection.

He's a grounded Virgo craftsman with lots of Uranus in his chart, reflecting his almost paradoxical desire for both Virgo routine and Uranian independence. I'm a "more intimacy please" kind of Libra, with a lot of intense Scorpio, combined with an edgy "let's go for it" Aries energy. It's not perfect. Yet with my North Node in earthy Taurus in the second house of "owning my own personal resources" I benefit when he makes me do things myself that I'd rather not do on my own. His Gemini North Node has lots of different interests that grow his Soul, and challenge him to be a better communicator. We talk more than before—he stretches to find the words and lingers longer in our intimate conversations. I let him know now when something is really important to me, but we do not expect so much from each other. The sting of how we hurt each other in the past did not leave the moment we re-married, but it's cooled and softened over the years. These days we delight in coming together at the end of our work days over some bowls of pumpkin soup I make and serve in his hand made pottery bowls. We remember things the other has forgotten in our mutual history, and we allow more room for "letting go" of what isn't truly important.

As an astrological counselor, I'm always being asked about the aspects and omens of love and divorce. When do we know its coming? When do we act, and when do we wait? It's a complicated question, and it's necessary to look at not only one's own transits and progressions to the birth chart, but also the comparison, synastry and composite chart for both people. There are no definitive "signatures" for marriage or divorce, and the chemistry created by two people is unique. It doesn't matter if you are a fire sign Aries, and your lover is a watery Cancer. Why? Because your Moon, rising sign, or another aspect could "complement" that emotional water element.

Unfortunately, there are entire books which will tell you what sun sign is good or bad for you, and what to "red flag" and what to go for—but I believe it's more complicated than Sun and Moon sign astrology. It does tell us some general things, just as knowing if a person is Italian or Swedish or their sexual orientation, or their age will all give us something. But it's not enough.

So when I'm asked specifically about what might traditionally be called a hard or good aspect between couples, I explain that astrologers today look for both *grace and grit*. Easy aspects and hard ones. Because the "grit" promotes soul growth and deeper understanding, relationships need grace and grit. Nothing is fated, and the charts are reflecting the chemistry of a relationship, so they hint more of the emotional feeling-tone one will be exposed to, but not the outcome. What is most important is the intention of the couple, their knowledge of themselves, and their willingness to make conscious decisions at the right time.

All the outer planets play havoc with relationships, and there are books enough out there to offer suggestions—-but here's some astrological indicators for you to consider: In a comparison of two charts, the two most difficult situations to deal with are aspects between Uranus and Pluto to the Sun or Moon, Venus or Mars. The reasons are simple: Uranus, the planet of individuation and rebellion, likes space and freedom, and the chance to "do something different." In mythology, Uranus is a rebel, and like Prometheus, it is willing to steal fire from the gods when necessary. It doesn't favor the kind of coziness that other archetypal energies can accommodate—nor does Pluto, the Lord of the Underworld and deep transformation. He isn't a comfortable bedfellow either. Uranus and Pluto aspects between two charts say that this couple is involved in a relationship of profound transformation, and if they can't take the heat, well....you know the rest.

If there is any "red flag" between two people's charts, I'd watch especially for Pluto aspects between couples. This is because there is so much unconscious obsessive-compulsive activity going on, that if everything isn't totally above board and honest, one person is going to feel deceived or betrayed. Pluto is an invisible archetype in mythology, and often describes unconscious destructive power struggles.

❧ ❧

It is the timing of things that astrology addresses best, as there are times to "make love and times to make war" as it says in the Bible. Planetary transits are all about timing. When you're having a transit of Saturn, Uranus, Neptune or Pluto to one of the angles of your birth chart, or to the Sun, Moon, Mars or Venus, then you're deep in the crucible of life change.

Each archetypal planetary transit calls for a different response: for example, when you're in a Neptunian cycle of your life, it's hard to accurately assess what you feel. Issues can be deceptive or not what they seem, so an astrologer will often caution you not to sign on the dotted line for anything just then. Whereas in a life-changing Pluto transit, where one part of you has to die so another can be reborn, you may simply have to sign on the dotted line and surrender to a divorce, foreclosure, or a health/surgery document.

When Saturn hits your personal planets, as it did with my husband at the time of our separation, you may feel quite serious, or depressed with low energy. That "energy" has gone below into the unconscious and is stuck around the complexities of the issue. (However lest we condemn the serious Saturn too much, I must admit that it was under an influence of Saturn to my Moon when I wrote the letter that began to reunite us, and it was when Saturn was conjuncting my North Node when we re-married. Saturn summons us to serious action as well as reflection.) In contrast, I was experiencing the impulsive transit of freedom-loving Uranus when I walked out the door of my house in a snowy blizzard and left my marriage so many years ago. Both Uranus and Saturn summon us to change, but they do it differently.

When people individually experience Uranus and Pluto *transits* they are in moments of deep change and renewal. But the red flags I'm most concerned about between two people aren't so much about the transits—that is, not about the changing times, but about when a couple has Pluto or Uranus in hard aspect to each other's personal planets in *their birth charts*. You see this in the comparison of two charts, of putting one chart within the other in a bi-wheel chart, allowing you to see where there's a conjunction, square or opposition to the "Other's" Sun, Moon, Mars or Venus. Those birth chart difficult aspects are the ones that give one pause to consider...I like what the poet Rilke said—some good advice to consider if the natal aspects between two people suggests too much grit and not enough grace—he said: *"And then the knowledge comes to me that I have space within me for a second, timeless, larger life."* It is this that we can look forward to.

∼∽

One thing that is noteworthy in this huge subject of relationships is to remember that the search for the "Magical Other" is often a search for the Beloved Self within ourselves. We expect too much when we yearn for the romantic "Other" to fill those inner spaces that only our relationship with our Self can do. The search for romance can be an escape from the calling of one's personal journey.

But then too, the journey to our "individuation" or the Inner Beloved doesn't warm our toes on a cold winter's night the same way a real person can do. Nor does it give our necks a gentle stroke after a hard day! Only a real person can do that, and that's no small thing.

Aside from the joys and burdens that "romance" carries in our culture, we all need relationships. However it is a sad psychological truth that what we do not know about ourselves (both the good and the bad in our *shadow*) will be projected onto the Other.

We all project our childhood wounding and longings onto each of our relationships to varying degrees. But since the Other cannot bear responsibility for what is essentially *ours,* our projections give way easily to resentment and power struggles. Working to heal a relationship is a powerful way to self-understanding, and fuels the Jungian process of individuation.

I'd like to end this chapter by moving away from my story and theories about relationship to some very practical thoughts for those times when the heart must wait—ideas for you to use during those outer planet transits when there are no Excedrins for the heart.

ॐॐ

When we see in our charts difficult transits, and feel the suffering they often entail, we need to remind ourselves that the Universe is not out to hurt us, but rather seeking to transform us—but it often begins this transformation by ruthlessly (such a Pluto word!) taking away from us the very thing we think we need most—love. Not only do hard circumstances erode our outer relationships, but they give us glimpses into our own "bad behavior" and leave us feeling less self love.

So what can we do when our wounds, our nastiness, our unloving feelings arise? As a counseling astrologer and as a psychotherapist, I am uncomfortable staying at the level of diagnosis without some prescription. So, I'm going to take off my astrologer's hat for just a moment and put on my therapist's hat. Actually I would love to see the two more integrated, with less emphasis on technique and prediction, and more on the use of astrology as a healing tool that moves seamlessly into the other healing professions. Just as chiropractors deal with more than just adjusting bones, astrologers too can prescribe as well as describe. As long as our bias is known—whether our *prescriptions* are flower remedies or a range of holistic ideas, if we share our knowledge openly, the client (or reader) can choose to take it in or not. My bias in a reading is towards the North Node compensatory medicine implied by the North Node sign and house, yet I'd like to share a few of the generic ideas that helped me with my "Venus affliction" that has been the substance of this chapter.

෨෴෬

The healing work happens first beneath the surface of consciousness, just like a physical wound heals from the inside out. We might be wise to tend to this wound in a very similar way to any other wound—here are some things to consider:

1—First slow down. When you are wounded you stop! I like to think of this natural impulse to slow down, as the call to go inward and begin to "cocoon."

Just as when you are sick you go to bed, so also, when your "heart is breaking" your energy flows inward to question and grieve, leaving you little energy for anything else. Give yourself a break, slowing down, and taking care of your basic needs: food, rest, and basic self-care.

2—Diagnosis: What do you have? Do your transits tell you anything? Is this the last wound of a broken relationship—perhaps the last pass of Saturn over your natal Venus? Or is it a Uranus urge for freedom and change that is pushing on the stability of your marriage? Maybe there's another way you could play this out? Or is this a confusing Neptunian warning sign, an "angina" of the heart? How do you describe the condition, how long have you had it, and how did you get it? The wounded heart often needs professional help with this, just as we sometimes need to see a doctor. But if this isn't possible, you can do some of this work with your journal and your astrology chart. Take out pen and paper and write it all down. The search for clarity is a good beginning, and the chart is a good Rorschach test even if you're not an expert astrologer.

3—Create a Treatment Plan for yourself—Apply something to calm the pain down. Go inward to find the healer within, and follow instructions! Engage the healing power of Venus. Beauty and order help heal.

Your own intuitive healer may say you've got to write it out, paint it out, cry or rage it out, or simply clean your house with a passion. This inner healer, speaking perhaps this time with the voice of Uranus, might ask you to do something radical—and if it's not too rash, do it! Example: you may benefit by getting away for awhile from your home or circle of friends—consider a retreat or vacation to some place where you can gain perspective. Even a day away, or something to break up familiar routines can help. Do you always end the day with a glass of wine and a book or movie? Let your inner Saturn as healer, inspire you to sign up for a class instead, or take yourself to the library—anything to let your psyche know that although things have changed, they are moving in new directions with new possibilities.

Consider the combination of Venus and Neptune. Reach out for help with life affirming things and beauty. When artist Georgia O'Keefe was suffering from heart-wounding depression early in her life she was delighted to discover how surrounding herself with color, plants, and bright light restored her. Could you repaint your bedroom? Could you change the lighting? Consider surrounding yourself with things that innately hold inspiring energy, or simply things you love. This could be allowing yourself things you've tended to deny yourself. Why not get yourself a cat, fresh flowers, a musical instrument, or whatever else you may have put on hold. (After my divorce, I hated the loneliness of my double bed. So I bought a large aquarium and delighted in creating a Neptunian underwater scene. I put this in my line of vision across the bed and lit it up at night.) I also had a little dog. You'll intuitively know what's right for you to do.

Next, get yourself a therapist, coach, astrologer, or friend (or all!) and tell your story enough till "the sting" is out of the story. You'll need to tell and re-tell your story until you can see it as one drama within the larger story of your life. Consider what lessons or insights can be gained and be open to the idea of how this experience can generate new possibilities for you. Move beyond shame and blame. Find out what was unconscious and invisible in the relationship. Could you look at a comparison, synastry or composite chart of the relationship? Where is Pluto? What unconscious elements led up to this? How have your expectations, fears, or anger created or irritated this wound? Where's Mars in your chart? You may not be able to see it all at first. Keep cleaning and poking around. It hurts, but you need to understand the part you played in this wounding so it won't be repeated in the future. During difficult transits we often regress to obsessive-compulsive coping patterns, so by admitting your anger and your less-than-perfect behavior, you cleanse the wound with a deeper level of understanding.

4—"Apply a clean bandage." The bandage is your attitude and your healing plan. It will be temporary and will need to be changed. Stick with your plan even when it's hard. If you re-expose yourself to your ex-partner you risk contagious anger and re-engaging in the shame/blame game. Is Mercury retrograde and more talk likely to be misunderstood now? If possible, don't expose yourself to re-infection or more wounding unless you're with a therapist who can professionally help you reflect.

5—Give the tender wound time to heal. Timing! So much of astrology is about timing. Protect your heart from the sometimes toxic "advice" of well-meaning friends, and resist the urge to expose your vulnerability to the world. But yes, you will sometimes break down crying in the produce department of your local supermarket. So be patient and pace yourself. Can you create some scheduled routines and "dates" in your week? (Saturnian structures help.) This could be as simple as knowing that every Wednesday night you go to yoga, and every Friday night you go out to dinner with friends, and every Sunday night you call your sister for a heartfelt talk. Perhaps part of your treatment plan is to go to the gym or out for a walk every other morning for 30 minutes. Engage Mars! Put the schedule up in a place you see frequently, and forgive yourself if you're not perfect. The wound is healing beneath the surface.

6—Find alternative "healing medicines." Here's where astrology can also be helpful. What other transits do you have besides this one that's wrecking havoc? What are the *good* ones? (Yes, I know we shouldn't use words like good or bad, but on a feeling level you know what feels good, and any transit has good in it. Look for it.) For example: Have you seen that your 9th house of the higher mind, education, and travel is being activated by Jupiter this spring? Could you take a class in Spanish and begin planning a trip to Mexico? Or that 9th house inclination to take that foreign language class could land you a job teaching English as a second language. What starts as your gladness turns into something that the "world needs." Look at your chart to see where you can play with new possibilities and also to see the length of the "illness." Like all wounding, full healing takes time, but we don't have to suffer constantly—there are times in healing that are full of light and unexpected epiphanies. We are regaining the sense that we are loveable and that we can love again.

Trust in the process—that's astrology in action for me. Or, as a Chippewa Indian sage once said it: "Sometimes I go about pitying myself, and all the time, I am being carried by great winds across the sky."

෯෧෨

Chapter 4.
The Astrology of Mid-life and Menopause

Between the ages of 42 and 59 there is a revolution in women's lives that doctors' call menopause. Astrologers have three names for it: the Uranus Opposition around the age of 42, the Chiron Return at 51, and the Second Saturn Return around 59. These three stages that span the entire menopausal experience are the rites of passage into our wise woman years. Like any journey they have their merciless moments of drama as well as quiet epiphanies. But how might menopause be different if these times came with an instruction manual like some of us received when we turned 13? "This is menstruation! Welcome to Becoming a Woman." How might it be different if we did get a menopausal map?

Astrology offers us the closest thing to a wise woman's survival guide of these times that I've ever seen, although the links between these three stages of menopause haven't been truly explored. I'm going to touch on this huge subject and offer a few insights, although the exact timing of these events is best explored with your own astrologer.

At the first stage of the **Uranus Opposition** we begin our journey by being slightly unnerved and restless. The body's electrical energy system begins to get revved up—fired up by new messages from our glandular system. Uranus rules the electrical circuitry in our bodies, and the evolutionary purpose of Uranus is to create change—our life opens up; we see new options and possibilities. Our culture calls these years "peri-menopause" but astrologers see this as the time when we begin to be more true to ourselves, and do things differently. We may be shocked because repressed aspects of ourselves and long-forgotten dreams now come forth and demand expression. The unconscious stirs as we hear ourselves speak raw and out-spoken truths in a way that startles even us. This is the same energy that makes us feel even sexier and stronger as we become serious truth-tellers.

Peri-menopause is powerful and underestimated, especially since it creeps up on us undetected. It's as if our internal "shit-detectors" are amped up, and we can smell a rat or hear a lie a mile away. At this first entrance into the menopausal journey it's time to consciously make new plans, craft new intentions, de-clutter our inner psyches and outer homes, and prepare for a new life. The Uranus Opposition is the first call towards what the Jungian psychologists call individuation; towards becoming who you truly are. Trying to maintain the status-quo at this time is the worst thing one can do. Let this be your motto: "Let's do something different."

As we move through our forties into menopause, it's as if we're being stripped of the Teflon coating of hormonal agreeableness, as we're being catapulted into a time of intense honesty punctuated with times of intense irritation. The worst physical culprits, such as loss of sleep and hot sweats exhaust us, allowing the emotional rollercoaster of moodiness to have its way with us. When we're awake and sweating at 3:00 AM, we may find ourselves contemplating the limits of sanity, divorce or freedom even when we have a good mind, a good marriage or good job—-or so we think, up till now. Reflecting and reframing our lives is best done at 9:00 AM with our best friend over coffee, when we can exaggerate our "wet sheets story" just enough to get a good laugh and a tender hug.

While the age of 51 is the average age for menopause to occur, the process that leads up to it is as powerful as the actual ceasing of our periods. This is the turning point into our wise woman years, and many of us find ourselves coming into our own power and personhood more in our 50's than ever before. We've already been experimenting and finding out what works for us and what doesn't. We've made changes—physically, emotionally and spiritually. We are keenly aware that our life is already more than half-lived.

As we move towards the Chiron Return at age 51, the electric and truth-seeking trials of Uranus link up with the archetype of Chiron. The changes we've made and the healing we've done stand us in good stead as we approach the time when our periods actually stop, usually around the time of the Chiron Return. .

Chiron can be seen as the mythological image of the "wounded healer." As we round the corner past 50, we've gained some experiences and wisdom that can be helpful to others. The mythology of the planetoid Chiron is fascinating to read. The essence of it is that Chiron, the mythological god who was unable to heal himself, becomes able to heal others. Through the process of experimentation and self-healing he learns how to become a useful mentor, healer, and teacher although he was never able to completely cure himself. Chiron is like all of us who struggle with menopause and its many cures in an effort to heal and be whole. We delve into new remedies and try out new lifestyles seeking to find physical relief and the best life, but perfect healing may allude us. We do the best we can as we struggle through it. Menopause is sloppy in all the ways of imperfection, but if we take good mental notes on our process we learn a great deal. We learn that change can be good and that open-heartedness and experimentation lead to healing. We find our way, and then we are able to help others do the same.

As we make our way through the fifties we begin to approach the **Second Saturn Return**, which comes for most of us around the age of 59. This Saturn Return is typically easier than the first Saturn Return at age 29 as it ushers us into our wisdom and Elder

Years. This third and last part of the menopausal journey is when any unfinished business physically or emotionally needs to be taken care of. We cannot afford to be lazy in our attention to what needs to be done at this time, especially caring for our bodies. If we put off that call to the dentist, it may not be long before we're calling the oral surgeon. If we don't listen to our body's messages now we may have some tough lessons with "reality"-that's Saturn's job.

But don't be too hard on yourself. We all have unfinished business—coping with aging parents, health issues, loneliness...there are old problems and perhaps new solutions. We may slow down a little, and others may say we look tired. This is the time when our culture gets us thinking about retirement, and we are shocked when we tell someone our age. Can it be true? Our mental image of this age is ready to change.

This is when we need to look deeply at the anatomy of our intentions. It is indeed time to see oneself as a wise woman and to act the part with quiet dignity. But do you have any great ambitions? Have you looked at what Jupiter and Neptune in your chart is whispering in your ear? Maybe you could aim higher in your intentions? Or is it just about losing weight and interior decorating? On your death-bed will you remember poignant moments doing volunteer work at the hospital or the time when you lost (and perhaps regained) fifteen pounds?

But what are the words in our hearts as well as our heads? Intentions and affirmations may find a "disconnect" if these two are not synchronized. For example, if our heart desires a new partner and yet we're aware that our habits and lifestyle leave no room for another person in our life, then chances are it won't happen. Or if we are still holding a powerful longing or resentment towards a past partner, where's the room for a new person? This is the time to avoid the seductive power of our shadow and avoid scenarios where we feel our old unconscious stuff emerging—our old tapes of "not-good-enough" or "nobody loves me." A reality check may be called for.

Someone once told me that a good suggestion for this time is to "sneak a little God into your daily chow." This means different things for everyone. And we need to add the Saturnian practicality to the chow as well—-a Muslim might say: "Pray to god, but tie your camel". Or we remember the old-fashioned phrase: "God helps those that help themselves." The gift of the Second Saturn Return is a practical wisdom combined with a more compassionate attitude, but you can't bring naiveté to it. It's time to get savvy. Saturn is the archetypal planet of reality that rewards in the long run for work well done, but who, as the Lord of Time, can bring delays and occasional moments of melancholy. We lose our naiveté, but gain a larger perspective.

Having just finished this third and last stage of the Menopausal Journey, I've found that I still feel the occasional hot flash of Uranus, the struggle with Chiron-ian experiments in healing, as well as enjoying Saturnian moments of sitting quietly in my chair journaling. I'm finding that there is a new sanity and serenity emerging in which my ego needs are relaxing. And I'm remembering that when I'm not happy it doesn't always mean there's something wrong—it may be that I'm in the **process** of getting something right!

The Second Saturn Return also ushers us into the age of the "Yoga of Generosity." We may find that our biggest joys come from having the chance to give whatever we can to all those "youngsters" under the age of sixty. Whether it be giving our time, money, or telling our stories, it's time to link the pieces together into a whole, sharing our wisdom with the story of the rough road of the journey. Remember that the difference between the boring old person and the one with the love and sparkle in her eyes is that she's done her homework of digesting her stories. She doesn't ramble or bore you. She's learned something from her life.

How do you do that? Many people find this a good time to write a short memoir in which you touch on the highlights of your life as a first draft. Then go back and find photographs that not only add a rich visual element, but may inspire a second draft, or a deeper level of writing. Some people use sketches or collage to express moments in which life was complicated and paradoxical. Other people simply find that the Saturn Return is a great time to begin psychotherapy again—-this time not for crisis, but for telling and integrating your life stories.

As you move through your menopausal journey you'll see the connections and the dropped stitches of meaning and healing along the way. You can make a point to take good care of yourself, aligning your heart's truth with the mind's intention. Then point the arrow of intention in the direction of your dreams and let it release. It's no "secret" since you've been doing the work and taking good notes. Chances are you'll find the Second Saturn Return to be a very pleasant surprise.

෨෧

Till then, be patient your menopausal journey as a way of holding yourself tenderly; you could think of it as a way of being "pregnant" with the new you that is being birthed. And if you find the hot flashes embarrassing, you could simply say "my internal thermostat is broken." But we know the alchemical heat within you is birthing something quite special.

Chapter 5.

Jupiter: Opening to Gifts of Grace, Opportunity and Talent

Where am I lucky? Where do I have talents I may not know about? Have I earned or learned anything in a former life that can help me now? YES! These are the questions I often hear, and there's a way you can explore this yourself without having to have private sessions with an astrologer. You simply need to find where Jupiter is on your chart. Jupiter, that little glyph that looks like the number four with an open top, is the largest planet in the solar system, and for you it represents the area of your life where you have an innate gift of grace and a unique opportunity.

Where Jupiter is in your birth chart, and where Jupiter is transiting in your chart and life now, is the area where you have built up karmic credit that you can turn into gold. *Jupiter is a capsulation or distillation of the North and South Nodes "gifts" which I believe we have earned through our actions in former lives, and shows where we are graced and where our "gold" is located.*

Gold? Alchemical/philosophical gold or money? Perhaps both. Where you have Jupiter is where you are likely to have abundance, opportunities, talent, faith, and expansiveness—which can easily translate into money. Jupiter was called "the old benefic" in ancient astrological texts, and its position and transits were always deemed lucky, and even somewhat protective. Today we also know that Jupiter has a down side—"too muchness:" too much abundance, too much faith (arrogance), even too much food—and therefore weight! But even so, with a little forethought it's not hard to make Jupiter work for you rather than overdoing its blessings.

If you're looking at your chart now, look for the glyph that looks like the number 4 done in fancy calligraphy, with that open ended top. It will be in one of the 12 sections of the chart's circle and will have a sign next to it. That sign describes how Jupiter works for you; what is its manner and style. So, for example, if Jupiter is in the sign of Aries, it will operate in a courageous and forthright manner. The sign always describes the planet like an *adjective*.

We are going to look now where it is located in your birth chart. (If you don't have your birth time, and therefore can't know the correct house placements, you can still learn something by using the sign your Jupiter is in, and correlating it with the house number—Aries then, correlates to the first house, Taurus to the second, Gemini to the third, and so on through the natural zodiac.)

స్గ్ ఆ

So your chart is a circle that is divided into 12 sections called houses. The sections of the chart start with house *number one* being at the position of nine o'clock , and go backwards around the "horoscope" with house number two being at *eight o'clock*...and so on through the twelve houses. Each house section represents a different sphere of your life and Jupiter is sitting happily in one of the sections! So if you will imagine your chart to be a clock, put your pen at the section of the circle that would be the hour between 8:00 and 9:00. This is the section called the "first house." The next section, going counter-clockwise (between the hours of 7:00 and 8:00) is the second house. Now write in the numbers of each section from 1 to 12 going counter-clockwise in your circle and note where your Jupiter is...it's like a map, and you've just found the gold.

Here's a short translation of what Jupiter in each area, or 'house' represents:

1st House: You have an enthusiastic personality, a warm hearted optimistic style, a sense of self-awareness, and usually good health. People tend to really like you, simply for who you are. Your ability to deal effectively and pleasingly with others will always be a part of your grace or "gold." This is a position where you need to guard against over-eating and drinking—instead, let your enthusiasm for life move you towards saying yes to abundant opportunities. Sales work, teaching, and anything where your personality makes a difference is favored work.

2nd House: You are likely to find that you have strong urges to make money and the willingness to take the financial risks that pay off for you. (If you haven't tried it, now's the time!) Jupiter here brings generosity of heart and an abundance of resources—you know the value of true wealth and need never fear poverty. If afflicted (ask your astrologer) you could go over-board in a fling of investing or spending, but generally, anything involving financial investments, public relations, and the arts are favored.

3rd House: Jupiter's influence here reflects a bright and savvy intellect that enjoys a mental challenge. Dare to share your opinions as you tend to be lucky in the world of communications—-teaching, writing, working with children, and journalism are favored.

Also consider working in your local area or neighborhood, and consider engaging your brothers and/or sisters to help you—they can be a benefit to you.

4th House: Your early family life and married family life are favored here, as you create a great home atmosphere. Your family roots can nourish you as you understand the world of feelings and the importance of family, home and emotional bonding. You benefit from women and your extended family. Psychology, real estate, interior design, parenting and home/ landscape design are favored.

5th House: Optimism, enthusiasm, and a creative flair are reflected here. Try your hand at acting, painting, singing—any of the arts are favored. There can be a tendency toward risk taking and gambling, yet you sometimes seem luckier than the average person does when it comes to those things.... and with a little caution you can do well on your hunches. Working with children and all self-expressive activities are favored.

6th House: Being of help to others comes naturally to you and you are good at it. Your generous spirit and willingness to work hard often means you're seldom without things to do—again don't overdo, either with work, or with eating and drinking. You will find you have talent in crafts, in communication fields, and in all the helping and medical professions. Your health is good, and when you help others, you empower yourself.

7th House: The challenges and rewards of marriage are an issue for you, and you usually benefit both emotionally and financially from being married. However, don't let your expectations of your mate keep you from "working" on the relationship, or you may find you have an abundance of marriages and partnerships. You prosper when you work with others, as anything you do "in tandem" tends to bring you luck and joy.

8th House: Financial gains through investment and inheritance is often indicated here. There's also sexual exuberance, and a certain luck and deep understanding in dealing with life's major transition points—marriage, death, religion, etc. Following your interest in spirituality benefits you. Psychology, investigative work, research, and banking are all favored. Building and using joint resources will tend to bring you wealth. Traditionally, Jupiter in this house would suggest "long life."

9th House: The imagination and intellect are stimulated and strong here, and there's a deep spiritual understanding of people and other cultures. Travel, international relations, religious/philosophical work, teaching, law, and publishing are all areas of gold for you. You have an adventuresome spirit and need to bring a sense of freedom and possibility to whatever you do. Teaching a language or a philosophy in a foreign country would tend to bring you "joy."

10th House: You've got dramatic flair and tend to be lucky in careers where you can stand out and shine. You've got both an enthusiastic and practical approach to most situations which gives you a successful edge in whatever you do. With Jupiter here you tend to follow your vision to the top of your field and you are steadfast and successful with your career. Politics, acting, management, and anything that puts you in the public eye is favored.

11th House: You have a great way with people, and know how to work successfully in groups of all kinds. Work on committees, take a political office, work for a cause you believe, and use your networking skills in everything you do. Friendships are rewarding and benefit you. Fundraising, social activism and humanitarian work are all favored. Keep adjusting your priorities, goals and dreams and use the internet and other networking tools to help you. Traditionally, you may tend to "blossom" later in life.

12th House: You've got an inner sanctuary in your psyche that brings you peace of mind whenever you turn inward. Jupiter is ruling your unconscious and can come up in all the areas of your life when you least expect it. Your keen mind has a philosophical edge to it that permeates whatever you do. Your work speaks for itself, so no need to be "on stage." The arts, crafts, writing, and the helping professions are particularly good for you.

This 'taste of Jupiter' is a beginning, but there's more to be savored and explored in this area—adding Jupiter to your North Node "medicine" is a great idea as long as you don't overdo it. Moderate with Jupiter. Meditate on the *sign* that describes your Jupiter. "Mine your Jupiterian gold" whenever you can, remembering that as long as you don't overextend in things in that area that Jupiter rules, you'll tend to be lucky in that sphere of your life—-for you've earned that karmic gold!

Chapter 6.

Saturn: Moving Through Times of Great Change and Opportunity; The Saturn Returns at Ages Twenty-nine and Fifty-nine.

"When an inner situation is not made conscious, it happens outside as fate." C.G. Jung

The Saturn Returns at ages twenty-nine and fifty-nine are times of great change and opportunity. And so, they can also be times of crisis. What do you think of when you hear the words: *"Know Thyself" and "Nothing in Excess"*? These were the words inscribed above the sacred oracular temple at Delphi, Greece. One might think that by understanding and trying to live by those wise words one might avoid the great troubles in life. Perhaps they help. Our understanding of these words changes as we age, but life often plays some nasty tricks on us in the meantime. Perhaps this is why folks who understand "just a little" astrology view the coming of the Saturn Return, at approximately 29 years old and 59 years old, with deep sighs. But then, a little knowledge can be a dangerous thing.

Saturn is the archetypal symbol of a way of being that slows us down and makes us take a cold hard look at the realities we've built up in our lives. It can feel like the voice of the inner critic. In ancient times Saturn was seen as the "old malefic" and its passage was viewed with some suspicion. Saturnian times tend to frustrate and delay—they feel serious if not melancholy, and then we are called to change! The word itself has roots in the idea of melancholy, timely delay, and the demands of a wise old elder.

However Saturn also represents the arrival of the harvest, and rewards us in the long run for our hard work and effort. It brings a good harvest if we're willing to wait. Its passage in a chart—especially at the times of the Saturn Returns, marks a time when we have an opportunity for deep change and life-renewing rewards. Not so bad!

There are two Saturn Returns that happen to everybody: the first is between the ages of twenty-eight and thirty, and the second, between the ages of fifty-eight and sixty. It's necessary to consult the ephemeris or your astrologer to find the exact dates for you, but the feeling of the Saturn Return permeates this whole time period. Astrologically speaking, the first return is when we truly come into our adulthood, and the second is when we come into our maturity or elder years.

Our culture sees the age of twenty-one as the time of becoming an adult—but not for the astrologically minded. For us it's twenty-nine. And you may get your Social Security at sixty-five, but it's at fifty-nine at the second Saturn Return that your true personal and social security comes up for review. Saturn Returns can be times of rough passage, or harvest, and they're usually a bit of both.

The good news is that although Saturn's passage in our lives may mark times of plain hard work and self-questioning, it's also a time when opportunities present themselves to be thoughtfully examined. Procrastination now seems like a bad idea, but quick change isn't in the air either. Perhaps the old lover has finally committed "the last straw" and you know you must end the relationship. You make the difficult break, and then accept an invitation to go out for coffee with a friend. New possibilities are discussed, but the leaden weight on your heart slows you down.. Or you've landed the new job, but the learning curve on it sends you home in tears for the first two weeks. But you hang in there. Or you're finally pregnant, but you're so sick you can't enjoy it.

That's the feeling of the first Saturn Return, but look what's coming! If you follow through with your new vision, you've taken the first steps towards a true new beginning. Saturn likes to create forms and structures and new beginnings, but not without strong foundations.

The first Saturn Return is often marked by these kinds of personal milestones. We move, marry, divorce, go back to school, etc. The navigational tools are twofold: you must take a chance now, and you must give it all you can. If you are willing to do that, you will be rewarded.

Saturn asks us "Whose movie am I in?"" and then challenges us to be the director and author. Wouldn't it be so much easier if we could just read some "manual to life" and have the ghost of "Christmas Future" come to us to show the way? Instead, we are called to become our own best "author-ity," to truly become the author of our life.

We're being asked now to re-write our personal life script with our own spiritual muscle. Not always so easy, especially when our life drama is full of people who no longer reflect who we really are and what we are becoming. "Letting go" is another key concept for this time

The human unconscious has ways of conjuring up people, events, and situations that challenge us to the bone. Psychologists sometimes call it projection, and we feel it as the remarkable synchronicity between what's happening in our inner lives with what's happening to us in the outer landscape—I don't think it's just an uncanny coincidence. At times it's as if we've conjured up whoever or whatever we most wanted to avoid—or attract—in our lives. It's as if the unconscious "hires" other people to play out parts of our life stories—this one is the boss, this one the victim, this one the unfaithful lover.

At the Saturn Returns you've probably "had it" with some of these people and situations and its time to write them out of the script of your life drama. At each Saturn Return we are challenged to take back our projections and to look at the drama of our life as our responsibility. It's too late to blame anyone anymore.

∂∾∾

The Second Saturn Return, in the late fifties, is also a time that calls for concrete actions in the real world, but it can be more subtle and occasionally more insidious. If we don't do what needs to be done now, we might not be given a second chance. If we put off our yearly physical exam or don't stop the spread of some nasty growth, it may be too late later. If we take a stiff upper lip attitude and deny the fact that "the job is killing me" it may indeed kill you.

As the body ages, depression and physical difficulties inevitably arise, yet as the body becomes less an object of vanity it's a chance for the Spirit to rise. This is also the time when we may feel an uprising of irritability as a few old habits or attitudes have the chance to rear their nasty heads again. This is because now is the time to cut them off—to be done once and for all with them. You may ask yourself: why am I dealing with these same issues again? The answer is: because you've almost resolved them. And the last straw can be the hardest. The hallmark of the second Saturn Return is that if you deal maturely with the old pockets of unfinished business you gain the gift that will last till the end—the gift of wisdom.

And how do you do that? Priorities need to be clearer, and metaphorical closets and basements cleaned. There is a need to look at what we feel disillusioned about and let the illusions go, lest these old ghosts feed on us and make us bitter. It's time to slow down and allow more sweetness and companionship into our lives, and to let the wild dogs of ambitious willfulness fight elsewhere.

And if we're going to be ambitious, we need to do it in a way in which we can bring the fruits of our life to bear on the project—such as returning to something we already do well but doing it even better, and mentoring someone as well. With an attitude of reverence, we develop wisdom, and as we acquire that, we'll be naturally called to "mentor", to pass along the gifts of learning and expertise, especially to the folks at their first Saturn Return who are truly stepping up to the plate now. Sometimes they are our children.

It has often been said that under strong Saturn transits one can choose between exhaustion and depression—-some choice! It implies that because Saturn is often about doing hard work in the real world that exhaustion is the better choice—- indicating as Mark Twain once said: "It is better to wear out than to rust out." It doesn't need to be so tiring. So what are the tools needed to successfully navigate Saturnian waters? Here are a few ideas:

1—*Be Discerning.* You are at a time now when you understand things you didn't understand even last year. Use your new wisdom to make wise choices based on clarity of intention. Dream into your future and discern the path through the woods. Here is where the quotes: "Know thyself" and "Nothing in Excess" become relevant. At these times there is a necessity to pull back from the excesses of your younger years and to know what you can and cannot do.

2—*Take Heart.* Find ways to reach out to others and be humble enough to ask for advice. If your marriage is in trouble, ask yourself the questions: Is the relationship the true source of dissatisfaction, or is it the repository of my own misery? How much am I projecting my insecurities onto my partner, and not taking responsibility or even listening 'with heart'?

3—*Go Deeper.* Superficial "all or nothing" solutions can be a quick fix and Saturn doesn't like quick fixes. No quick decisions: instead, hold the tension of the opposites and conflicts within yourself till you see the emergence of a new idea. Then, and only then, is it time to stretch beyond your comfort zones to new places of thought and action. As was said so many years ago:

"Dig deep; the water—goodness—is down there. And as long as you keep digging it will keep bubbling up." Marcus Antoninis

4—*Take Action.* Saturn ultimately rewards those that act and depresses those who procrastinate. In ancient texts, Saturn was sometimes seen as a devil who made a hand signal that said: "All that you see, is all there is." That's the devil's lie. Prove him wrong.

ॐ ॐ

So Saturn can be seen as the spirit of Father Time, passing through our lives at these transits and "Returns" in the way Scrooge experienced his encounter with the Spirits of the past, present, and future. The purpose of these visits wasn't to give Scrooge a bad case of nerves, but to give him a second chance at life. He saw himself differently; he grieved, he tried denying and avoiding, but ultimately he _acted_, and propelled himself—just in time—into his new life. ⸰

Character, Destiny and Fate: Do It Now!

"When I was younger, so much younger than to-day, I never needed anybody's help in any way. But now those days are gone, I'm not so self-assured, now I find, I've changed my mind, I've opened up the doors."

Sound familiar? The Beatles wrote those lines in their song: "Help" in 1965 when they were in their twenties. These lines convey part of the underlying theme of both of the Saturn Returns: Help! Life feels different now and reaching out for help at the Saturn Return might just be the wisest thing we could do.

Each Saturn Return, one at roughly age twenty-nine and the second at fifty-nine, marks the entry into a new life, a life where we're going to be able to help others. And yet ironically, the transition in these years almost always feels like a rite of passage where we're more inclined to say "Help!" rather than "Can I help you?"

Help? Many people at these ages, as well as any-one going through strong Saturn transits, may be surprised at the subtle, yet fierce changes in their lives now. There's an insidious clash that takes place during Saturnian times between the acquired personality and the demands of the true Self—not the self you've grown into becoming in your life so far, but the newer version of the Self that is struggling to find its place in your world. It's as if you may have been trying to fit into clothes that were too small or simply not right for you anymore, or the feeling of living in a house that's too big with rooms that are never lived in. Saturn passages are the times when we change the outer appearance and inner structures of our lives to make a better fit.

An Insidious clash takes place? That sounds threatening, dangerous and unconscious. And I've carefully chosen those words because I've come to believe that this unique time period is different than what I previously believed. It can be as quiet and personal as an "attitude adjustment" or as silently serious as a brain aneurism or stroke.

All rites of passage carry a dangerous feel to them yet the nature of this transition often looks easy unless we find ourselves not listening to the warning signals of the body and soul. Around the time of the Saturn Returns people often say: "If I had only listened to my body and lost that extra weight before I had the......" or "If only I had realized how deep my resentment was, I might have gone into therapy first, before divorce court."

Saturn strikes us where we have unfinished business. The outer world doesn't know our inner business and we may have learned such excellent coping skills that even our best friends don't know what's happening with us. Everyone has some regrets, wounds, betrayals or lost expectations and illusions that still need to be compassionately dealt with—and this is the time to do it.

Saturnian times tend to hold some melancholy as the word "Saturnian" implies. But astrologically, it is also a call to action in the real world. This is time when we would be wise to ask for help with our soulful introspections, because after the first whiff of melancholy has passed, we realize that what is facing us are very do-able changes, and we certainly don't need to chastise our self or to metaphorically "knock the house down" when all we really need to do is to add a small room of our own.

So what's your unfinished business? What do you say when people ask you how you are doing? What if how you say what you are and how you're doing is not what's really happening? How much would people smile, if after they asked you how you are, you just looked them squarely in the eye and said "I'm in the middle of a serious attitude adjustment just now..."

There's an inner shift; an earthquake of varying intensity happening within most people who are enduring Saturn transits. The first Saturn Return appears to change the outer life in more drastic ways, and in my experience, is simply more stressful. The second Saturn return can actually be rather quiet and inner oriented.

These two Saturn Returns that transform our psyche could be described as a shift from the holding of youthful illusions and magical thinking to a more grounded mature movement of the Soul towards its own destiny. And of course, all this happens both consciously and unconsciously. Sometimes for example, it could mean a shift from holding onto a romantic illusion of falling in love with a "magical other" to learning to truly love the people who are in our lives now. Or we might reconsider what "loving" means for us, and what form real love could take in our lives.

Another word to consider here is "destiny." This is a strangely vague word—it's different from "fate" which implies pre-ordained. Whereas *destiny* comes from the Latin verb "destinere" meaning to determine, and implies making choices—in Greek, the etymology of destiny is "proeiroismus" which means to flow within relatively fixed but still changeable boundaries, as a river may flow. Whereas fate is derived from the Latin noun, "fatum" meaning "to speak of divine law." Here we have something outside of our ability to influence.

So destiny is a verb that implies choices and determination. (And how interesting too, that we make our choices so often based on desire, which means "of the stars" in Latin. As my friend Jim Hollis says, "Desire helps us guide our ship across the wine dark sea." But who can read the stars correctly anymore? Most navigators do not rely on the stars to guide them, but instead it's the astrologer who now looks up to the heavens above for counsel. And I wonder, how many astrologers can accurately read what is written there?

☙ ❧

Back to Saturn—ask yourself: what is my unfinished business that Saturn wants me to attend to? What hidden attitudes or hidden agendas are still creating a destiny that has unhealthy unhappy patterns? What is the default story I tell myself about "how my life is?" Am I still overcompensating for feelings or beliefs that aren't true anymore?

Carl Jung believed it's a complicated question because this unfinished business is most likely coming from a part of our nature that we don't often pay attention to—in fact, we avoid it. He said that neurosis is about the suffering of a Soul that hasn't found its meaning, and that our suffering comes from trying to avoid the true struggle with the issues that we are *destined* to struggle with. So avoidance, procrastination, and distraction are the true devils here.

What's complicated too is that we are always pulled in so many directions by the various voices in our psyche: our inner committee. There may be a Self/Soul that is constant and central, the chairperson, but it's surrounded by a committee of various archetypal characters who each have their own agenda and lobbyists. They each clamor for dominance and attention like the different planets in our birth charts that pull and oppose and square each other. The Sun as the committee chairperson tries to give balance, integrity and time to each of these parts of us, and the North Node is like the messenger with the unconscious contract for this life. But do we listen?

What are we to do? Why not give ourselves time to truly listen? What if we listened to all the voices, all the planets, and took good notes and prioritized our needs based on our deepest values. How would we be different? It's not an easy thing to contemplate—most of us are afraid of the answers, because we still base the locus of authority outside of ourselves, whereas at Saturnian times we are called to be our own best authority—and there's nothing frightening or judgmental about that.

I recently heard a story about a woman who was in her Saturn Return who was talking to her new therapist about all her problems. The therapist was overwhelmed at first by the physical, financial and interpersonal pain this woman was suffering, and was yet surprised by how well she seemed to be coping with it in spite of all the confusion. When the therapist asked her client how she managed the woman answered, "Well, when my body hurts I ask it what it needs, and I listen. And when I'm lonely, I ask what my heart needs to be happy, and I listen. And when I can't pay my bills, I think about ideas I can come up with...and I listen." The therapist knew from her willingness to ask herself these questions that she was going to do well, and in fact she did make her way through this transition time successfully.

That dialogue with the Self is the essence of Saturn transits. We all have certain unique problems at each stage of life, but it's our willingness to take the time to honestly dialogue with our own conflicting desires and opinions, rather than running from them that makes the difference. If we are to open up to the largeness of a life to which we are being summoned, then we need to pay attention to our internal promptings—or as astrologers would say, to our planetary archetypes and their changing functions.

At the Saturn Returns, the archetypal energy of Saturn is more likely to ask us now—how can I be more self-sufficient, and how can I help the world and those I love? At the first Saturn Return, we are meant to help ourselves gain a workable ego and a place in the world. At the second Saturn Return, we need to shift our emphasis from building up our life, and an ego to be able to handle it, to the quieter requests of the Self.

෨෧

As we move through the passage of each Saturn Return it's a great time to say "Help, I need somebody!" Like in the Beatles song, the two Saturn Returns herald us into new levels of subtlety and challenge. Having lived through lost illusions and betrayals as well as successes, we must now afford ourselves the time, energy, money, and whatever resources we have to ask ourselves: "What do I really value now? What is life trying to tell me at this point in my life journey? Saturn, like the old good teacher that he is, may feel intimidating at first, but like a wise teacher, he brings forth the answers out of ourselves and rewards us for asking and for being motivated. He reminds us not to let the obstacles of this next phase of life get us down—"illegitimus non carbarundum" he might say: "don't let the bastards grind you down." And then he'd turn and walk away with a smile on his face...

Openings in the Curtain of Fate; The Interweaving of Saturn and Uranus

In a few months I'll be turning sixty. I'm shocked by the word "sixty" and all its implications, and I'm shocked by how I look before that first cup of coffee in the morning. Being part of the "Pluto in Leo baby-boom generation" I'm a classic of that type: I still act and feel young and resist the undertow of aging in every way. Being an astrologer, I'm motivated to look at the mid-life transits of aging again and to glean what I can about these changing times. Is there life beyond the Second Saturn Return? Something to look forward to from the astrological perspective?

What's next? What about that Uranus square coming up at around 63? And then the Saturn square at 67, the opposition at 75, the square again at 82 and finally the Uranus Return at 84? And beyond that? Is there life—or is it the art of dying—at another Saturn opposition at 90? Of course there are other planetary cycles, but the oscillating patterns of Saturn and Uranus—of contraction and expansion, of constructing and deconstructing, are intriguing—have you noticed that there's three Saturnian "events" to every one Uranus event? After the Uranus Opposition at age forty, Saturn opposes and squares itself three times before Uranus comes knocking on our door again. What's that about? Maybe something's happening here that isn't obvious.

ॐ◈

We know that Saturn is about the urge to create form, to make a foundation, and to build slowly and carefully a structure in which to contain a part of our life. Whether it is the slow process of building a house, or being pregnant, or writing a book, Saturn demands time and patience. And when something isn't right, there will be delays and discomfort. The good news about Saturn is that when we do what must be done—when we do our "homework" we are rewarded. Saturnian times often feel contractive and limiting, but they are do-able; we can focus, make an effort, and usually see the fruits of our efforts.

Uranus is about change; often unexpected change. It's the archetype of the inner rebel and it expresses the urge to break free from some of those Saturnian structures and self-imposed limitations that we've created. Although Uranian times seem to arise without warning, and feel shocking, they are ultimately liberating, and are a release of the tension which has been building up over time. Uranus breaks down and breaks through—it allows us to feel free and start afresh. It allows for radical aliveness, and is known as the planet of individuation.

ॐ◈

One could look at the interplay between these two planetary energies as the interweaving between doing and being. Both energies engage us in a process of self-creation that seeks to hold our *be-ingness* and *do-ingness* in balance. This idea is central to the philosophic concept of Existentialism.

The existential concept that "existence precedes essence" was the motto for those French Café Existentialists of the fifties, such as Jean Paul Sartre and Albert Camus. They revolutionized the world with a concept that moved their readers to inquiry into the nature of freedom and structure in their lives. The existentialists challenged people to not just accept themselves by their roles, their sexuality, their nationality, or whatever external structure, but instead to take more freedom (Uranus) and responsibility (Saturn) into their lives and to live their full potential. The existentialist's 3 word formula was: existence precedes essence. To claim that existence precedes essence is to assert that there is no such predetermined essence to be found in man, and that an individual's essence is defined by him or her through how he or she creates and lives his or her life. As Sartre puts it in his *Existentialism is a Humanism*: "man first of all exists, encounters himself, surges up in the world—and defines himself afterwards."

It's been said that Existentialism is now the true religion of the world, because no matter what your metaphysical beliefs are, most people *practice* the existential religion of personal self-creation. We make our identity and reality, just like we "work" and make significant choices in our Saturn transits. This working and choice making allows for what those philosophers called true authenticity. Astrologers might consider the intertwining and opposing pulls of Saturn and Uranus *the fuel* for the urge for authenticity and individuation. So no matter how disruptive or anxiety provoking the freedom of Uranus can be, or how heavy the responsibilities of Saturn, one can hope that not only are these energies fuel for the journey but also part of a divine plan to help us become all we can be. I believe it is so; yet I don't believe we can understand the justice or karma of one life alone—I think we would have to see it amidst the backdrop of many lives.

So as we age, there is a dilemma here—we sense that we are coming up to a last chance to do something. Serious ambitions can arise. Saturnian concerns for security and structure move in. And yet as the body loses some of its "sovereignty" there is a natural tendency to feel depressed about what we can no longer do as well as before. We may have to work harder during the Saturn Return so that we can get a chance to let go and BE later on.

This dance between Saturn and Uranus, like the tension between doing and being, can inspire us to see that the time is soon coming to relax the needs of the ego to prove itself, and to explore the mystery of what is beyond the small story of "self". The doing, constructing, and reflecting aspects of Saturn set the stage for the radical aliveness that Uranus ushers in. Uranus transits draw open the curtain of fate and allow us to say, "Here I am, this is really me, like it or not."

These interweavings of Saturn and Uranus feel like a call of destiny and a call to action in the real world. They feel personal and in-our-face, as well as metaphysical. Their transits are as much a crisis of the spirit, as a crisis of aging. We know that if we resist the constructive building and "taking out the trash" aspects of Saturn and resist the need to rebel and liberate ourselves in Uranus times, we're going against the nature of the transit. And when we resist the natural order of things, suffering happens.

So Saturn calls us to look again, to redefine, and to slow down—it can depress us too, if that's what it takes to make us re-evaluate ourselves and do what must be done. But Saturn transits give us the time to make the do-able changes of letting go of superficiality and to move into a more real life. It always asks us to find our inner authority, and with that a deeper authenticity in the world. It calls us to set the stage of our life.

So it's after Saturn has "worked us over" through the inner squares, outer oppositions, and the "knock you down and bring you around" conjunctions, then we are ready for the Uranus transits. We've done what we could; now Uranus gives or takes away that which is no longer needed, or creates an unexpected twist in our life drama. Uranian transits have the "aha" quality of synchronistic grace when they're good, and the inevitable mark of fate when they're not. They're irritating, exciting, and life changing. What we sometimes forget is that although they can be edgy they can also be a great adventure.

∂∽∾

I've decided that after this Saturn Return is over, I'm going to look forward to the Uranus square at 63. I don't know what will happen then, but I have a feeling I won't have to try so hard at my "doing" or care what someone else thinks about how I'm "being". I can feel it coming. Perhaps it's implicit in the work of the Saturn Return itself, though I can't see just how it will work out yet. However I'm setting the stage now, creating my focus, and leaving the curtain of possibilities open for Uranus to enter.

And so at sixty-three, I might just be ready to take things a little less seriously and have more fun. I might even find more joy in Saturnian pursuits, whether it be the soft pleasures of grand-parenting or writing a memoir or mentoring....and the Uranian "aha" may be about buying or building that new house that is finally the right size and in the right place—even if it's across the country. Or instead of working or traveling more, I might just decide to travel "inward" to the terrains where I can be in pursuit of the mystery of Self. I'd like to explore more deeply into this dance of fate, character, and destiny. And all that feels very good, and very alive. ~

Chapter 7.

Uranus: "We are Constantly Invited To Be Who We Truly Are."

"If you think you're about to fall, point your hands in the direction you are going, and dive gracefully. At the very least you'll inspire someone watching you." E. Spring

Henry David Thoreau once noted: "We are constantly invited to be who we are." ***Uranus transits are that constant invitation.*** And whether you're falling down, waking up, or dancing to your own drumbeat, there are times when you may wonder—isn't there a different way to do this? 'Diving gracefully' is always a good option if you are falling, but there are times when if you want to soar you're going to have to break the rules. These periods of Uranian liberation are a call for you to do that! Break your own rules—challenge your status quo.

'When I'm sixty-three'...or twenty-one, forty-two, or eighty-four years old, something rather magical happens—or can happen. Uranus transits happen to everyone at approximately these ages, and we live out these times *optimally*, from an astrological perspective, when we savor the changing opportunities and sometimes shocking epiphanies rather than trying to maintain the status quo. It may feel like we're falling or coming apart, but these Uranian ages are truly opportunities to *soar* and *dive* rather than collapse. These are the years of radical new beginnings that give us the chance to become more of who we really are.

Uranus transits are times when we are called to release our grip on the Saturnian status quo that we have created in our life, and it often feels like the low rumble of an earthquake approaching our solidly build structure. Not a pleasant feeling unless you are an excitement junkie. So something begins to create anxiety, and we can see it as the call to change and exciting possibilities, or we may simply feel it as fear. Something has to de-construct in order to make room for us to re-construct. The whole house doesn't have to fall down, but now we may remember how long we've procrastinated moving.

Astrologically, it is at the times of Uranus transits that we can feel safe in saying *yes* to change, and safe in allowing our *inner rebel* more freedom. At these ages, and whenever Uranus makes a strong contact in your chart, you are wise to accept the idea that the road to safety is through change. You must "dive or soar" now or the Universe will cosmically arrange a "fall" or disruption of some sort. Most of us would prefer to be proactive, and so I'd like to offer the suggestion that you follow your inspiration and intuitive "inner rebel" now and go for it. You have nothing to lose that can't be lost, and everything to gain.

In this way of thinking, the Universe is ultimately kind even when seemingly destructive. And if the earthquake destroys the house, let's hope that your new beginning awakens in you potentials and adventures you never dreamed possible.

Of all the Uranus ages and transiting times of change, the Uranus Opposition that happens to everyone between the ages of 39 and 42 is the strongest. Let's rate that one at least a five on the Richter scale. The Uranus Opposition is an extremely transformative, exciting, and unnerving time—it's a great time for a "reading" or to begin psychotherapy, or even just to keep daily journals—why? Because this is the time when you truly get a chance to re-invent yourself and to pick up the threads of dreams you've tucked away till now. Most of us need a little help and encouragement with that—especially if it should mean a radical change of job, partner, or changing an old habit that has limited us.

Although it's a bit simplistic, we could say that we respect limits during Saturn transits and break limits during Uranus transits. And although the natal position of Uranus in your birth chart is an important reminder of the constant call to awareness and change (in the part of the chart Uranus rules) the *transiting aspects* are the call to change NOW.

Look to see what area of your life—what house— Uranus rules in your natal chart and look to see where it is transiting now. The natal position is where you were born with divine dispensation to break the rules. One might even say that you are not only given permission to do things differently in this area of your life, but that you must do things differently and authentically here—you are called, in this area of your life, to be radically honest and a little more daring than ordinary.

For example, if you have Uranus natally in your birth chart, or by transit, in the Fourth house that rules your home and family, there is a subtle divine imperative that you rebel against your family of origin in some way, or change something in your "home, heart and hearth." It could be as simple as a change or rebellion in the way you tell your story about *how it all is*. You don't have to make changes dis-respectively and you don't have to stop loving and communicating with them. However, you are called to break the rules of the *family myth* here—as the family myth may sound like this: 'Isn't it funny how all the men on this side of the family are bi-polar?' Or "Isn't it funny how all the women of this family marry abusive men?"

When Uranus moves through your fourth house you probably have heard some variation of a 'not-so-funny' theme like this handed down the family line and you're going to need to make a conscious effort to break this family legacy.

For you to survive spiritually there are times when you need to learn to stand up to authorities and separate yourself from what has been culturally ingrained in you. You may think you are already aware of these influences and that you did the work of rebelling against these cultural imperatives when you were 21—or before. Yet it may have taken you to the Uranus opposition around the age of forty, to realize how deeply you were programmed to be a certain way. Maybe it took that long for you to divorce the wrong person you married, to find your vocation instead of your job, or to reclaim your natural love for music. Uranian times call for you to reclaim aspects of your Soul you've put on hold, and to challenge yourself and rebel against your own assumptions about what's right for you.

Radical acts of reclaiming ourselves and daring to break the rules can happen at any age and are specific to you alone. However, it's almost as if the Universe gives you a chance for enlightenment or liberation at those ages when Uranus metaphorically "turns the lights on and off" in your life. What was going on for you at the Uranus waxing square at 21? The opposition at 42? What could happen at the waning square at 63 and the return at 84?

At 21 years our culture says we are now an adult, but in fact, most of us have been in school or in less-than-empowering positions for most of this time. Our parents and the culture have exerted pressure, overtly and covertly, to mold us into something. Now we have the first chance to say: "but this is now my time and I want to find out who I really am." So we summon our courage—often with the help of our peers and abundant sources of alcohol—to dare to move out on our own into whatever may await us. But it's usually not untill we're close to thirty, and have the first responsibilities of true adulthood—at the first Saturn Return, that we commit to a deeper level of our truth and make major and usually sobering 'Saturnian' life-style changes. But that's only part of the story.

∂⋙

In the process of living our adult lives, parts of us never get a chance to be expressed. In order to raise the family and/or pursue the career, we live our lives with parts of our essential nature sacrificed. We tell ourselves that some day we will take up singing/painting/writing again, but at the moment we remind ourselves that we have to work two jobs, perhaps raise two children and make enough money to pay for the cell phones as well! Priorities are what count—we need to honor our commitments and our ongoing responsibilities, but perhaps ask ourselves—where is the wiggle room in all of this for the Self to be honored? Where can I give myself the personal time to honor my deepest desires? Do I even know what they are anymore?

When we approach forty, the awareness comes to us that we're at mid-life and we're closer to our death than our birth—-and by forty the lights have been blinking on and off just enough to remind us that if we're going to do 'it' we better start now or we may never do it at all. So we have the first classic mid-life epiphany of waking up to the preciousness of time. Many people will marry, divorce, move across country, or take up 'guitar playing' at this time. Others will need to make time to rediscover what part of their Self they have put on the shelf and consider if its worth the effort to reclaim their forgotten ambitions or unacknowledged joys.

So at the Uranus Opposition there is often anxiety, restlessness, and a desire to be rebellious against what has held us in check. We may be shocked by how liberated we finally feel when we act on what appears to be impulse. But that impulse has had years of pressure building up behind it. And yet if we should miss this chance, we get another chance for living our deepest truth at the waning square of Uranus at age 63. We may have thought that the time for new beginnings has ended. Not so!

It's worth taking a moment to think of what makes 'an elder' an interesting and vital person. What gives charisma to an older man or woman? Could it be that they don't care so much about what other people think about them any more? This Uranian attitude is one part simple acceptance of themselves and others, and one part 'detached wildness.' This quality of wildness looks more like a wide smile and a quick laugh than a purple hat with a red feather.

At each of these Uranus cycles—at 21 and 42 and 63 and 84 we get a new chance to answer the voice within us that calls for more unique individuality. Even at 84 when Uranus returns to its birth position, there's a part of us that opens up to ways of seeing things differently. Personal epiphanies abound at age 84 and people often notice a renewed sense of well-being and a feeling like a "breath of fresh air has come into their lives". Some people, such as Carl Jung and Joseph Campbell *completed* their lives at this time.

The closeness of death itself stimulates us to recover our core individuality. You are being called at these Uranian ages to allow a radical honesty to arise within you, and to take up the 'yoga of doubt and questioning' and turn questioning into 'questing'. Being true to yourself requires courage, but life helps us as we approach these 'Uranian times.' You don't have to know all the answers and figure it all out yourself. These are the times when you can expect help from the Universe by the occurrence of unexpected events—unusual feelings, new opportunities, and paradoxical situations. Not all will be pleasant, but the effect will be to move you to the next stage of your life journey.

Uranus transits are times to answer inner restlessness with a 'Yes'! Try something liberating and freeing—make a little noise; cause a little havoc, give up trying to be too self-sacrificing. (If a child is always 'too good' don't you become suspicious? What is being repressed? Why are they saying they're bored?) At these ages you have a 'divine dispensation' to break the rules—so ask yourself: how have I allowed life to dampen my energy? What's inhibited me? What still resonates and stimulates me when I think of it?

Einstein once said: 'God doesn't play dice with the universe.' I don't think God plays dice with us either, and no event is without the potential for using it for creative liberation. The writer George Eliot wrote: 'It is never too late to be what you might have been.' Experiment with that idea, and let your mantra be: 'Let's do something different.' And if you should fall or fail...well, as I said earlier: 'point your hands in the direction you are going, and dive gracefully. At the very least, you may inspire someone watching you.' But chances are, you'll soar.

Chapter 8.

Using Neptune Homeopathically; "Spiritus Contra Spiritum"

"Similia, similibus, curantur."
Latin: "Like cures like" by S. Hahnemann

Last night I awoke in bed at 3:00 AM to find myself struggling to name that familiar ache in me that has no name—that core pain that sometimes sits heavy on my heart. I thought about all the times I've felt it: my childhood homesickness that hurt so bad it felt like a toothache, my adolescent struggles to separate from my mother, the unrequited loves of my twenties, the sense of loss before my divorce, and the various pains of betrayal from friends through the years. They all have a theme: separation from a place of togetherness. Of all the aches in the heart, that particular pain of separation, yearning and disillusionment—of an unlived or ill-used Neptune, may be the hardest and the most illusive of all pains.

I say "illusive" because the depth and scope of Neptunian pain is so often permeated by illusions and its healing can defy rational analysis. It's not that its causes aren't clearly evident it's more that the *cure* for Neptunian problems may lie precisely within its own realm, and respond best by homeopathic thinking.

As we know, Neptune is about the urge to merge and refers to permeable boundaries and those things that don't separate us. It can be the longing for a lover, a philosophy, a true friendship, or even a better way of living. It's that part in us that longs to transcend the daily routines, to let go of differences and "flow with the waters of life." Neptune yearns for divine love, and despairs at how human love so often falls so short of the ideal.

❧ ❧

In Neptunian times we often react to the pain of disillusionment and separation by wrapping ourselves in a fog of self-deception and addictions. We're confused. Romantic illusions, painful melodramas, glowing sunsets with morning hangovers, and the larger-than-life spin we put on the stories we tell, are all in Neptune's oceanic realm. We play out the merging and imaginative qualities of Neptune either positively or negatively (and often both at once) depending on how it's aspected in our birth and transiting charts.

When we fall under the spell of this mythical sea-god we need new medicine. The same astrological culprit that created our feelings of separation, loneliness, or disillusion can be the one to cure it. "Like cures like" say the homoeopathists. Neptune cures Neptune. This homeopathic remedy uses the inspiring qualities of Neptune to cure its disease.

എസ്

But first you might ask: Is Neptune strong in my chart now? Everyone has Neptune somewhere in their birth chart "doing" something, but it only gets activated at certain times as it transits across the sky and aspects your chart in a particular way. If you don't have your chart or astrologer to help here, you could ask yourself: Am I generally "high on life," inspired, idealistic and at times naive? Yet do I struggle to maintain the feeling that life is as it should be and that I am all I can be? Do I see both sides of the question when it comes to decision making? Do I feel the pain of lost loves and friendships more than most people you know? Does even reading this article make me ready for my evening glass of wine, even though it's only noon? If you've smiled knowingly to those questions, then Neptune is playing a prominent role in your chart and life now.

So how do we use Neptune homeopathically? Or simply said, how do we cultivate the higher octave, the wisdom of Neptune? Carl Jung delved into this when he said: "Spiritus contra Spiritum." This Latin quote is what Jung said to the founder of Alcoholic Anonymous; essentially it is only "spirit that can counteract spirits." Jung felt that all *adult* neurosis originated from our separation from the meaning making function of Spirit. He saw how we tend to literalize spirit, and drink it instead as "spirits." Alcohol eases the existential pain of our separation from our spiritual nature briefly, but it isn't the cure.

Surely we can nourish our self with all that inspires us, and renew our connection to spirit in whatever form that takes for us. We can take ourselves to the ocean for inspiration and baptizing by her waters, or enjoy a glass of wine at the end of the day, or do its literal opposite and not have the wine, but join AA instead, and find a community of like-minded spirits. Or we meditate and read books that speak to our Spirit and attend "spiritual rituals".

Ironically, some of these things can be especially hard to do in Neptunian times if we're feeling very disillusioned. In India, the Hindu's have a spiritual saying for that: "neti, neti"—meaning "it's not this, not this," implying that we find our way to what is true and healing for us by finding what is not—by finding what is illusion, false fear, and needless drama, and then letting it go.

Jungian psychologists deal with this problem by saying we need to hold the tension of the opposites within us, without trying to deny or escape the situation. In the "holding" of the situation we create a container, or crucible, for alchemical energies to create change and transformation. One is encouraged to hold the despair or the unsolvable situation till the third "numinous" option appears. Jungians suggest we wait till there's an opening in the veil of maya, the opening between illusion and disillusion. Astrologers too, also usually counsel waiting during a Neptune transit, and caution clients to not "sign on the dotted line" during these times.

Waiting is an option, as synchronistic events will often appear and lead us where we need to go. However, for those of us who like to be proactive, or use the homeopathic idea, then we can use Neptune itself to solve Neptunian problems. Here are some very practical proactive ideas for doing that:

First, consider the benefits of "breaking your own narrative." Neptunian reality is a story we tell ourselves about how it was and how it will be. Is it really true? Would it be seen differently by someone else? How would it be for you if you didn't hold onto your beliefs about your story? The subconscious is very suggest-able and the stories we tell ourselves about "how it all is" go deep. Much has been written about how we can monitor our thoughts to avoid repeating the same old tapes in our head that feed on the low ebb of self-esteem. At these times we can replace the tired stories of our life with ones based on new insights as to why things happened. You can find new seeds of inspiration and retell the story of your life with a new slant! You can choose to see how the universe has co-operated with you to give you what you needed, not always what you wanted.

Second, could you use your Neptunian gifts of visualization to dream into your future? As Jung said: *"Your vision will become clear only when you can look into your own heart. Who looks outside, dreams; who looks inside, awakes."* Practice intuitive strategies on yourself based on what only you—or your astrologer knows about you. Only you can read between the lines of what you say and think. Neptune represents our ability to use our intuition and to know things about ourselves that others can't know rationally. One can't say "yes, but" to ourselves indefinitely, before we realize that we need to dig even deeper into our psyche to take more responsibility for our lives. Neptunian dreaming ignites the urge for change. This is good medicine.

Third, could you use this "spaciousness" or the open-minded fogginess of a Neptunian time to let go of tight expectations of ourselves or others. Get a little looser. At these times we stand on shifting sands of illusion and can unwittingly deceive ourselves and others without meaning to—for example, we may give affection and attention when we don't really mean it, or simply make poor decisions. Instead we could give time to exploring new ideas, people, and plans that are tangible and will hold up in time. But, as any addiction therapist knows, one of the hardest things to do in treating an addict (read: a rough Neptunian transit) is the recurring sense of despair that comes with a realistic outlook. We need to dream "high enough" to excite us, yet be grounded enough to find sources of true support in hard times.

A last consideration: Neptunian energies need thoughtful release not repression. Don't let anyone tell you to keep your dreams or your despair under wraps, yet there's a need to differentiate between sheer outbursts of grief and acting out indiscriminately. We don't want to be "dry drunks" in any sense of the word—people who live their wounds, drinking or not. When we enter into the experience of our Neptunian-separation pain, we would be wise to bring some reflection and containment on the emotions we want to express. Could we search for the name of what truly ails us? And if we can, could we express it through a poem, a song, or a nurturing talk with a good friend? Could we use it to counsel someone else with a similar pain. In all of these, we are using the feeling of yearning, longing, and disconnection to fuel us to connect with Self. Neptune curing Neptune.

છે ન્

Here's an example of how this process can work. A woman I'll call Catherine called me for a reading when she was on the verge of a divorce. She had already separated from her husband, and as she talked I began to feel that what she wanted to hear from me was encouragement to finalize the divorce. She wanted to "sign on the dotted line" but there it was—transiting Neptune squaring the Sun, and it still had over a year to go in that position. I had to counsel her to wait, to endure a state of not-knowing and to look for new sources of inspiration. I could tell she was quite depressed and not happy with my response.

The next time she called, she sounded a lot better, and was happy to tell me that in her "waiting" she had gone for a massage when she was at her lowest ebb of feeling. While under the nurturing hands of this therapist she felt revived—both by the subsequent massages and her new friend, who encouraged her to start attending massage school. She picked up on this new inspiration and loved the school, although she said that the waiting was still hard and her teenage son had started acting out in school. She didn't know what to do with him. I again listened and had to counsel continued more Neptunian homeopathy.

The third and last time I talked to her was just after the Neptune aspect had passed, and she had good news—she was just graduating from massage school, felt less financially fearful, and her husband and son were respecting her in a new way for all the hard work she had done at school. Even her voice sounded lighter as she told me that as part of the divorce mediation process, she and her husband began seeing each other with new eyes! They felt their mutual love for their son was acting as a bridge for them to truly hear each other for the first time. Because they hadn't signed on the dotted line, their marriage was getting a second chance. Her son now was having his own Neptunian problems with alcohol and we brain-stormed ideas as to how he could find the connection to spirit that suited him best. The Neptune homeopathic remedy we felt might work for him was to encourage and support his love of acting; a Neptunian art in which one enters into the spirit of another person and works with others to create an entertaining illusion.

There are many ways to use astrological homeopathy, and it's particularly effective with Neptune. When planets make strong aspects by transit we need to honor them by "feeding them what they need" which is simply to act out the higher octave of their very own nature. This works for all the planets. Neptunian homeopathy calls for dreaming into the future and a re-visioning of our lives as well as finding new ways to deeply reconnect with our Self, with others, and Spirit. Neptunian transits appear to be subtle times, but in truth they are very potent times—reach for the highest octave of the sign, and be careful what you wish for as it may come true. Neptune knows how to wish upon a star...

Chapter 9.

"Pluto's Ruthless Orchestration of Fate; "Called or Not Called, God is Present."

Pluto's transits have everything to do with what makes you feel really crummy—you feel as if you are "falling apart." That's the way it strikes *at first*. Sickness, divorce, moving house, changing jobs, the Uranus opposition, and mid-life "menopause" (for men and women!) can all fall into that realm. Although the feeling of weariness or even death is metaphorical most of the time, you still feel it in your bones—this *dying and being re-born sensation*. The phoenix-like nature of Pluto is powerful and ultimately purges us of our worst habits and karmic weaknesses. It appears unwarranted and uncalled for—just plain unjust and unnecessary, but apparently the "orchestra leader" has a different idea for us.

The first part feels destructive and disintegrating because it has to "tear down" before it can "build up." Just like when a contractor goes into a neighborhood and tears down a house first before he can build a new one—it doesn't look so pretty at first, but it has to be done that way. So Pluto brings up, irritates, and hopefully heals those **South Node default patterns** we've been discussing. It ultimately changes things for the better—or at least on our deathbed we might say "it changed things for the better."

"Ruthless" is a word that is commonly associated with Pluto, partially because it seems so unbending in our efforts to change it. The really difficult moments of transiting Pluto are when we feel the hand of fate moving through our lives, and changing—without our permission—the orchestration of our lives. That's why the words *surrender* and *let it go* so often come up at these times. We deal with Pluto best when we allow ourselves to let go of every image we have of "how it all should be and look."

When Pluto comes into your life by *transit*—that is, when it hits a *hot spot* in your chart, such as conjuncting or squaring your Sun or a personal planet, you know something's about to undergo a metamorphosis. The ego is usually under attack in some way, or the part of your ego that is tied up with your South Node complexes. Most people feel overwhelmed and "attacked." As you ego fragments under pressure, your inner voices start screaming and it's easy to *project* those attacking inner voices onto other people. We regress and lose our maturity at these times, and there's nothing to do but *endure and trust the process* until there is a moment of palpable shift and insight. There will probably be *many* of these "attacks and insights" or regressive acting out times followed by little "Ah-hah!" epiphanies. Whew! It can be quite tiring.

৯১৯

Pluto transits are long, often lasting a couple of years, and they have two parts: a deconstruction/de-integration phase and a reconstruction/re-integration phase. The first part of the transit involves this disintegrating phase—sometimes this deconstruction part, if it's not resisted, can simply feel like the closing of one chapter of your life. The reconstruction part is where we open the new chapter, and it can be like having physical therapy—we keep at it because we know we're in a healing process—we endure and hold on. Examine your South Node shadow, to see what you can do and where you could possibly take on more responsibility. And, this is the time to look at your particular "North Node Medicine" and use it.

৯১৯

Wherever the South Node and Pluto is located in your birth chart points to an area of deep karmic wounding, and from that wounding there evolves a behavioral distortion or a complex. We

all have this in varying degrees. **The good news is that when we have a Pluto transit, or a powerful transit to our South Node, we get to revisit this at some level, and to make it better. In a sense, we are getting a chance to be** *reborn.* **We can often feel the sense of fate; the hand of God orchestrating all this, and so it actually brings us closer to God, our life purpose, and what the Jungian's call "the transcendent function." The suffering involved is a high price to pay, but ultimately worth it. The less resistance we offer, the less suffering there is. As Buddhist author, Pema Chodron once said: "Suffering is optional."**

$\approx \sim$

So when you see this transit coming, you look at the planets and houses involved, and get a sense for what area of your life will "be reborn." But before you let out a huge sigh, let's ponder this a moment...

Pluto holds the potential for great healing and renewed personal power—and **there's a secret that Pluto holds.** Yes, you can skip to the end and get a quick look, but it you can take a couple of minutes; let's start at the beginning...

$\approx \sim$

When you think of the word 'alchemy' do you think of obscure etchings in ancient books where the alchemist-astrologer hovered over a crucible seeking to distill the philosopher's stone? Do you remember how he was supposedly trying to find the meaning of life by transmuting lead into gold? **Astrological symbols infused these strange images that were meant to both teach and conceal teachings that were thought to be too advanced for the ordinary man**. But we have an advantage. Because we understand the language of astrology we don't need to be an occultist or of royal blood to apply what they thought was esoteric—we can translate the abstract texts and practice real alchemy in our lives.

The ancient alchemists knew that there was power in transforming the base metals—or the base emotions—into gold. Whether it was the melancholic Saturnian *lead*, or Plutonian 'shit'—that modern term for all that is dark, disagreeable and trouble-making in our lives—they knew that if we didn't transform it, we would project or transmit this negative energy to others, laying the blame on them. And the results would not be pleasant. **Simply put—one transforms or one transmits.**

Surrendering to the process of transformation is one of Pluto's key secrets. We need to willingly submit ourselves to the transformation rather than resist it. And if we can gather up whatever *trust* we have in the process our life, and in the astrological saying that "this too shall pass" than we are better prepared to submit.

So if fate, through the hands of Pluto, is going to transform us, then our response to this summons is really quite exciting. We have power in our response, and here's where we need to look again at the higher octaves of our Nodes and say "now is the time."

Let's take an example: let's say you have transiting Pluto conjuncting your Venus, or your progressed Venus conjuncting natal Pluto. Similar situations—but what's Pluto going to do with this? What's love (Venus) got to do with it? Quite simply, we have to look at **what happens when we put desirous Venus together with Pluto; God of the Underworld.** Uncomfortable bed-mates for sure, but like Persephone and Hades, very powerful.

We know Venus is about beauty, love, and the striving for harmonious relationships and Pluto is the uncontrollable urge to go deeper and to transform. The Venus way of desire is the positive yearning for something, and has a sweet flavor. We can deal with the juicy desires of Venus without complaint, but the deeper realms of Pluto are shrouded in unconsciousness and are seldom dealt with pro-actively. They happen to us through all degrees of unpleasantness, yet still we remember that the Universe is not out to hurt us. It's just that most of us don't change till the situation gets very intense! Plutonian circumstances seem to come at us from others—or from external circumstances—-and force us to look at what we don't want to look at and 'corners us' into making a change.

Pluto's favorite stomping grounds are relationships, and not the easy ones—the ones that matter—the ones that stir your ambition or hormones or survival urges. So whether we're talking about Pluto/Venus aspects or simply *any* Pluto aspect, know that it's going to enter the relationship realm at some point. Relationships can be life transforming and we enter into them willingly because we are drawn by the chemistry or the possibilities of the encounter. And though you may be thinking of 'good sex' here, it's also about deep friendship, relationships with your brother or sister, and even the relationship you have with your boss that hints of possibilities not included in the employee manual.

So, two of Pluto's ruthless swords are envy and jealousy. The good news is that envy is the highest form of flattery. You wish you had those "looks," that position, that relationship, or that house. And it may make you uncomfortable to see your *lack*—can you admit that? But the high road here is to use this feeling as a guide-post, a wake-up call, and a directional map. You don't have to go unconscious and drop into the resentful emotions of jealousy. Instead you can choose to embody and be that which you desire—you can follow your destiny. And yes, you might just need to *have* what it is you feel envious about! But before you despair and argue that it can't happen; think about it—it doesn't mean that you must have that *particular* person, job, or educational advantage specifically—-but you can have or become what it very deeply *symbolizes* for you.

Here's where even a little understanding of alchemy can help. In relationships, and in particular in Venus/Pluto contacts, what needs to be understood first is who's right or justified in the situation, right? Who's got the most 'shit'—right? No. Pluto has come along because something was old or stuck or rigid and needed to die and be reborn.

Pluto doesn't care who is right or wrong—it is simply ruthless in its demand for change, reform and rebirth—and it doesn't care if you are the innocent party or not.

And because Plutonian feelings are so unpleasant we all love to point the finger of blame somewhere. Remember that the central law of projection is that whatever is unconscious will be either repressed or will "show up" in the other person—maybe even at your therapist or best friend for not warning you that your lover acts like a jerk most of the time. Projecting the blame may ease your conscience, and may be completely true, but it doesn't make the pain go away. Something is dying; and eventually a new birth will take place. The labor is never easy.

But you *can* get the good feelings back and reclaim your Soul. If you want to have a relationship with Mr. or Ms. Unattainable or have whatever Pluto has taken from you, then you've got to play at the level of Pluto. Suffer the lack of it. Feel and see what it is you desire. Name it. Pray and sing and swear about it. Then wait, and let die whatever is holding you back from "getting it." Then you reclaim **yourself and your power** in a new way.

You may feel like you're dying—but don't stop at the death part—keep going and make the little changes, and wait without hope. Hope at this point, might be hope for the wrong thing. Just do what needs to be done. Take that 12 step program or weight loss plan or go back to school, or do whatever you need to do to bring the essence of what you desire into your life. Move into the labor, knowing you are birthing. Know that you are coming into your power and that you are creating that which you most desire.

Part of the alchemical secret is in the knowing that it's not always about the *literal* object of your desire. Alchemists would say they were looking for gold, but it wasn't the literal gold they wanted, although that would have been an acceptable by product.It's also about what is behind the person or thing and how it all makes you *feel*. And there are many ways of getting at that. Use your desire—your Venus energy—to make the connections to other people and a new way of life. Create a transforming new crucible by eliminating what is not essential to your highest purpose. Release the old pattern, person or situation in whatever way you feel called to, and begin to get slowly out of that stew.

It won't feel good at first to let go of what you've been obsessing about. But here's where 'the Secret is'—and it's an old Jungian concept that is indeed a miracle. Now Carl Jung wouldn't call it that, but I will. You've got to hold the tension of the opposites, the pain of the situation and <u>wait</u>. You need to hang on the cross of your own suffering and simply wait—holding onto the awareness that you see no solution right now. But as you hang there, feeling the impossibility of it all—and not trying to escape to a quick addiction or release, you will eventually see the appearance of the "the sacred third." A new idea/feeling starts to arise. And as you begin to sift through the muck you'll now be able to distill flickers of insight there. Use them to fuel your new actions and new life! Then you'll be well on your way to understanding what the "philosopher-alchemists" knew—that what does not destroy you makes you stronger—and that nothing has the power to destroy your essence without your consent. But the secret is in the waiting...

Chapter 10.

The North and South Nodes: Our Soul's Messengers
"When an Inner Situation is not made Conscious, It Happens Outside as Fate."
C.G. Jung

"The Nodes are the single most important point in the chart—they describe what your Soul wants to learn and experience in this life. They are the Soul's Messengers."

On my desk, and on the cover of this book, is an "astrolabe"—a globe-like open sphere with two circular orbs connected by an arrow going right through it. In Medieval times, these strange little spheres with their roman numerals and astrological signs were used to make astronomical observations. It was a navigational device. Today, as I see it "glowing" there on my desk, I think—this is it! The arrow shooting through the astrolabe is like the North Node in the astrological chart pointing to our personal North Star.

In ancient Indian Vedic astrology this North Node point was called "Rahu" and the base of the arrow, the South Node, was called "Ketu." The astrolabe's encircling spheres have a little ball right in the center of the arrow—reminding me of that Mystery that is our Self. The arrow itself is like a soul messenger pointing to this North Star Node—showing the South from where we came, and the North to where we are going.

The image of the astrolabe pulls all the details and confusion of the astrological chart together. The chart itself is a guide, but often such a confusing one to synthesize. Within each of us are so many "voices" in our psyche, and so many paradoxes. And then there are so many theories on what's important astrologically. It's simply hard to know what to prioritize in our charts. For me, the Nodes contain the most important and the most unconscious karmic parts of our evolutionary journey—I honor them as alchemical gold. .

So what are these Nodes? The Nodes describe the evolutionary needs of the Soul—-the North Node describes what your Soul yearns to go towards—what it longs to learn and experience in this life, and what compensatory actions we can take to make our lives better. The South Node tells a story about the past; about the influence of heredity and karma, or simply the "default" patterns we fall back on when we're not being conscious.

The South Node is usually understood as what we didn't get right in the past, the unfinished and unhealed business of either previous lives, or our early life, or even the family genetic tendencies. It describes the personal karmic habits we've come into this life with, and which we are now ready to grow beyond. Yet there's "gold in the shadow of the South Node" as well—for just as we inherit negative traits from our family and personal past experiences we also inherit the good traits as well. And because we inherit goodness, or "gold" in the South Node, we can give to others what we innately own and understand. Vedic astrologers say we "feed others" through our South Node. As we access the higher qualities of the South Node and offer what we know to others, we also benefit by "feeding ourselves" by stretching towards the North Node qualities. Are you with me so far?

The "Nodes" answer questions of soul purpose and life direction—-not from the perspective of ego and personal ambition, but from the Soul's perspective. For centuries, astrologers overlooked the message of the Nodes in their search for sun-sign predictions, and Indian Vedic Astrologers viewed the Nodes *not* as auspicious, but "malefic" influences. Perhaps in India, change in itself was viewed suspiciously. In a time and culture where there had been little free choice and mobility, people felt un-empowered and learned to accept their fate. Predictions reigned, and free will was questioned.

Now these old malefics are seen differently, and are sought after sources of knowledge about who we are, what we may have "brought over" from a previous life, and where we're meant to be going in this one. So the North Node, originally called the" head of the dragon" and South Node, "the tail of the dragon" have emerged out of Indian astrology and mythology to offer us clues into our past patterns and future aspirations.

Today the Nodes are perhaps the most controversial and debated aspect in astrology. It has been a great mistake, in my opinion, for astrologers to have written books where they *combined* the sign and house position as if they were one, because they are related but not the same! Signs describe the planets and the Nodes; the houses describe in what sphere of your life the "action" is happening.

There are an increasing number of books, websites, and blogs dedicated simply to understanding and deciphering the Nodes. There's a great curiosity about what these points can tell us, and there seems to be no end of debate over how far we can—or should—try to excavate their esoteric meanings. As the psychologist Carl Jung once said: "When an inner situation is not made conscious, it happens outside as fate." The Nodes are a tool to help us change fate to choice, unconsciousness to consciousness. There's great mystery here, and we seem to be bravely drawn to explore this mystery—to look at our shadow selves and to make conscious what has before been before kept secret.

అ✍

Have you ever wondered what life-lessons and experiences your Soul wants to have in this life? Do you know what you truly yearn for? Do you worry that your mother's "personality disorder" or your father's alcoholism could be inherited the same way as you've inherited your grandmother's red hair? This ancient astrological technique of examining the North and South Nodes offers profound clues into these questions. Combine these clues—these *suggestions* from the Nodes—with a little astrological savvy, and you've got "a message from the gods."

So what are these Nodes? The Nodes are not heavenly bodies, or planets, but are a mathematical point based on the relationship between the Sun, Moon and Earth at the time of your birth. The Moon's Nodes are where the Moon's obit around the earth intersects with the "apparent path" of the Sun around the Earth...the ecliptic. Astrology's frame of reference is the earth (geocentric) even though we realize the Sun doesn't orbit the earth. The Sun and planets do not circle haphazardly around the Earth, but in a disk-shaped path as seen from our frame of reference on Earth. The Moon's orbit around the Earth is like a hoop, with the Sun's path, as we see it, creating another hoop through the heavens. Where the Moon's orbit crosses the ecliptic in two places, these are the Moon's Nodes. Astronomically, the moment-to-moment position of the Nodes "wobble" up to a degree and a half—not usually enough to make a difference in a chart. So most astrologers use what is called the calculated *mean node*.

The Nodes create a polar axis—that arrow—and they are always in perfect opposition to each other. So if you think of the Nodes as the places where the Solar and the Lunar orbs connect, it underscores the primal importance of the active principle of the Sun and the reflective principle of the Moon, and how important they are in "a reading." When it comes to understanding the chart, the Sun, the Moon, and the Nodes are the holy trinity.

❧✦

Now if you take a look at your astrology chart, you'll see that the North Node is a glyph that actually looks like headphones or a little doorway. It could be seen as a cosmic doorway through which we would be wise to pass through, since it hints at qualities of character we need to emphasize. It offers insights into how we can move past our comfort zones into new territories—-territories that we are not always comfortable or familiar with, but which contains our "growing edge."

By contrast, the South Node looks like a reversed doorway, or a horseshoe with its ends pointing up. It describes what we've brought over from our youth, from our parents, and from our previous lives—if you believe in reincarnation. Or more simply, it can be seen as our default patterns, reflecting our deeply habitual and ingrained ways of being and thinking. In times of stress, you'll fall back on your South Node habits because they are so very familiar, but they don't help you move along in your life. A better direction and soul purpose is contained in the "message" of the North Node.

The South Node holds what Jungian analysts call the *shadow*: the negative and repressed qualities that our Soul wishes to move away from—-some people might be inclined to see it as our downfall. But the Swiss psychiatrist Carl Jung was wise enough to recognize that there also is "gold in the shadow." When we uncover and use this goodness or gold in the shadow of the South Node, while leaving behind the negative old patterns, we move into playing out the higher octave of possibility here. This gold is often the unrecognized and repressed talent that is latent in our psyche, brought over from a former life.

Astrologers and Jungian psychologists would argue that we don't truly access the positive potential in the shadow of the South Node until mid-life, and it is then that we can begin to "feed others" with what we've learned from our past. Jung reminded us of this change in our life when he noted that we cannot live out the afternoon of our life in the same way as we've lived the morning. He felt we truly come into ourselves at mid-life, not before. Astrologers point to the 18.5 year cycle of the Nodes around the chart, noting that it takes 2 revolutions of the Nodes around the chart to bring us to age 37, which was about the age that Jung felt that the real process of growing into our true nature begins—-the process he called "individuation."

So the South Node reflects the unfinished business and challenges that we didn't "get quite right" either earlier in this life or in previous lives. As the gateway of the past, this nodal door opens onto what has been sown before; the karma of the past and it is where we tend to retreat when challenged. Gold or no gold, there's a lot in the shadow of the South Node that needs to be eliminated. But because there is gold in the shadow, we benefit by knowing our family karmic inheritance—both the positive and the negative traits and secrets that have been handed down the family line. This is discussed in the chapter on the family karmic inheritance.

The foundation of the theory of the Nodes rests

on the concepts of karma and re-incarnation. However, if you prefer not to think in terms of karma and reincarnation, you can think in terms of the unrecognized gifts and challenges brought down the family line that you've inherited from the parental DNA. You can also think of karma as simply being the law of cause and effect. The root meaning of the word karma means "action" and it isn't too far of a stretch to see how the "actions" of our early lives and of our parents and grandparents might have influenced our current life now. It isn't hard to imagine that we "karmically" learn from both our mistakes and theirs. One can simply see the karmic story as "what goes around, comes around" whether it be in this one life, in many re-incarnated lives, or in a family over generations.

When the Nodes are understood in the light of re-incarnation, they are said to reflect the story of the original Soul intention on coming into this world. In this viewpoint, the Soul progresses through a series of lives growing in experience and wisdom until it returns to the original Oneness. The South Node shows the mistakes that have been made along the way, the lessons that weren't quite learned, and the suffering that ensued. Because the South Node holds hints of your past life experiences and the North Node speaks to the direction your Soul longs to go towards in this life, then a link of cause and effect creates a karmic pattern that gets imprinted on the Soul and this story is embedded in the chart. Some astrologers also flesh out details of a "past life parable" by examining the rulers and aspects to the Nodes in great detail.

&∞&

So how does this all work together in a chart? Let's look at my chart as an example. My North Node is in Taurus in the 2nd house, and South Node in Scorpio in the 8th house. What can we understand about that South Node being in Scorpio in the 8th house and its Taurus polarity? If you look ahead to the chapter on the Scorpio/Taurus polarity you can read about it in more detail. But generally, the Scorpio South Node has connotations of dramatic life changing experiences, power struggles, sexual bonding, and other people's money and resources—suggesting that my Soul purpose is to move away from hurtful power struggles, melodramas and to ground myself in *my own* talents and resources. The Universe gives me strong hints whenever I move into territory that is not my own to claim anymore. The Taurus North Node speaks of the desire for serenity from the drama and trauma of what came before, and the need to not re-peat the dramatic excesses of my earlier years and/or former past lives.

I've worked on acquiring the qualities of loy-alty and persistence of Taurus, and keep reaching to find the "sacred in the commonplace" which is such a beautiful quality of Taurus. Early in my life I did this by becoming a potter and I suspect that the "gold" in my Scorpio shadow/South Node is my intuitive ability and emotional empathy that I now use as an astrological counselor. Scorpio, both sexual and intense in nature, has its "snout to the ground" in order to find out what undetected emotional truth is happening in any given situation, and so Scorpio is the sign of the investigator, the truth teller, and the shaman. Taurus, on the other hand, loves ownership and being grounded in the sensual things of this world. Taurus is the Earth Mother (or Father) who bakes fresh cookies for the children, and knows exactly how much money is in the bank—although she may not want to think about it!

Until I came of age at my "first Saturn Return" at age 29, I acted out my South Node by stubbornly learning things the hard way, by being ungrounded and going to excess. I had an intense longing for the kind of perfect love that no human could ever fulfill. Not surprising, I married late, and after 20 years of marriage was divorced for five years, and later remarried my husband. We've been married now for eight years, and continue to do the wonderful and horrible work that soul mates do with each other: we help each other grow. I can see how he naturally pushes me to live out the independence and grounded values of my Taurus North Node as I encourage and stimulate the curiosity of his North Node in Gemini. There's grace and grit here—-what I'd call a true marriage.

But what about that South Node in the intense and dramatic sign of Scorpio? It tried to seduce me in every way you can imagine. As a child of the sixties, I found myself in sexual and powerful relations with other people who were in positions of prominence. Because that South Node in Scorpio was also in the 8th house of other people's resources, I suspect I was repeating a past life scenario of being the person who was the "power behind the throne" or the woman who basked in the glory of the one who was out there doing the work. (In the chapter called "Going Deeper" you'll see how the house placements of the Nodes add more dimensions to the nodal signs.) Earlier in my life, I also sensed that as long as I lived in the reflected light of other person's glory, I would only feel a temporary high. I could feel that something was inauthentic in my life, but it took many years for me to learn a craft(s) and then a profession in which I truly followed "my own God home."

It's significant too, that I have no earth planets in my chart—-except the North Node—-and so perhaps I was unconsciously drawn to compensate for this by developing a skill in pottery making, and then choosing to live in an old stone house, and marrying a man with lots of earth signs in his chart. One could call that the "pull of the North Node." It's as if the North Node in earthy Taurus had pulled me first to compensate for the lack of earth—Jungian psychologists call this the unconscious compensation of my inferior function; the sensate, the earth element. Then, as I became more grounded in a stronger ego, I was able to retrieve the gold in the shadow of the South Node and study the "Scorpionic" and spiritual realms of astrology and psychology.

These days, I continually recommit to ever deeper levels of grounding and persistence in my work and life. I find that astrology reflects the internal dialog between the sometimes paradoxical parts of my nature, but now I know which "voice" in my psyche is the wisest—that North Node.

A chart can never be interpreted once and for all, but needs to be looked at over and over again, just as we look in the mirror to see how we've changed from day to day, year to year. And what is the value of predicting the next upcoming "event" when the original Soul purpose is overlooked? All the planets in the chart are karmic and tell a story, and there may be an important full Moon, eclipse, or grand alignment of *whatever* going on in the heavens, but if it doesn't aspect some planet or sensitive place in *your chart*, then it's not as likely to affect you personally.

The Nodes, like all the transiting planets, move around the birth chart in a timely manner awakening us to new possibilities—they make a full cycle around the chart every 18.5 years. When the Nodes and planets hit a sensitive spot on our charts it's as if the planet is summoned into your life for a "tune up." However it's the signs and positions of the ***birth nodes*** that never change and this is most important. The meaning of the birth Nodal axis is what pulls it all together. It can take a life-time of observation for the symbolism of the Nodes to reveal its secrets.

৵৽

So now you may be wondering about how "your sign" fits into all this—how your Sun sign relates to the Nodes. You could think of your Sun sign as the *vehicle* which your Soul has chosen to utilize in this life. The combination of your Sun sign and your North Node reminds me of a make and model of a car: like Toyota/Camry. Ok, so maybe you've chosen a vehicle for this life that reads: Libra Sun/Taurus North Node. That says a lot. The Sun describes the personality/ego/self that's coming into its true Selfhood. The Nodes hold the more subtle description of the vehicle and the directional log for the journey. It hints at where you've been and where you're going—holding in its cryptic way, the most important piece you'll need to know to navigate your journey home.

৵৽

Now it's time to take a look at what I call North Node Medicine: finding the sign of your North Node, and reading its description along with its opposite sign, the South Node. Then, if you have your astrology chart in hand, you can expand on the story by looking to see what section of the chart (the house) that the Nodes fall in, what aspects it, and what "rules" the Nodes.

It's like *a puzzle* you put together—here are the signs of the Nodes, here are the houses, and here are amplifications of that story through aspects and rulers—we can get pretty detailed here, but the deeper you unravel the clues of this journey, the more room for greater intuitive insight, but also error. It's best to think symbolically and metaphorically rather than literally, and *to find the places where the pieces of the puzzle overlap and repeat*—that's where you'll find your truest story.

If you really understand the basics, and the subtleties of you Sun sign and the Nodes, then you have a great map for your Soul journey. Let the understanding grow over time. And as you move through your life passages—your transits—you'll have a reassuring guide in hand, in a soul language you can understand. You'll then know the conscious story of your personality and Sun sign, and the unconscious soul memory that is *embedded* in the Nodal story. That's powerful, and indeed good medicine!

Chapter 11.

North Node Compensatory Medicine, and the "Gold in the Shadow"

At the first reading of your North Node Sign you may be nodding your head in agreement, and then thinking: Well, isn't that true for everyone? Yes, if something is deeply true, then it is true for everyone. However, each sign has a particular truth that rings truer for you than for others. All the North Node "Medicines" have a *particularity* to them through their sign and house position, and a potency that is activated by that particular polar dynamic. The prescription, like a vitamin, might be good for anyone to take, but it's really only necessary and highly effective if you have the symptoms and the chemistry particular to your own Nodal nature.

Here's an example: Let's compare 2 sign/house placements: the sign of Leo which naturally rules the 5th house, and Pisces which rules the 12th house.

I think of Leo and the 5th house as "the house that Joseph Campbell built." Why? Because he popularized the phrase: "Follow your own bliss." This is good medicine for those who have their North Nodes in Leo or the 5th house because they both point to *self-expression and open hearted generosity*, as well as all the joyfulness and creativity that comes when we become as little children again and just *play*.

North Node Leos, with their South Node past in Aquarius, have had childhoods or past lifetimes when they were separated from this particular kind of creative, loose, joyful play—they could have been exiled, persecuted, a genius, a role-model (one who had to be a good example!) or one who didn't quite fit in for some reason—they could have been ill or restrained in some way, or they may have placed duty above personal expression and joy. They come into this life having forgotten what playing and self-expression can do! Now there's a soul yearning for this person to come into the group, into the circle of love—through intimate relationships, children, artwork, or just having a good time. They are being summoned to simply follow their own bliss.

Let's compare that with the "House that Carl Jung built"—the 12th house and Pisces. If you have a North Node in Pisces or in the 12th house, you are being summoned to explore the world of the "collective" and the unconscious. But how can consciousness enter into unconsciousness? We can enter that world indirectly through dreams, divination, active imagination, and by noticing moments of synchronicity between what we're feeling on the inside and what's happening on the outside. This is Jungian territory. We are called here to go beyond traditional boundaries into the Neptunian worlds where the mind and the heart join, and where mysticism and psychology meet.

This is not for everyone. But if your North Node is in Pisces or located in the 12th house, then there is something for you to gain in exploring these worlds. There is healing medicine for you deep in your psyche, and you have been given "cosmic permission" to seek Oneness with this world. This is an area where we are not duty-bound, not having to be "right", and not having to march to anyone else's drummer. You are simply and quite mysteriously being called to become aware and conscious! Some might say you are called to be enlightened. Some might say you are called to peek into the" in-between lands" where fate, destiny and character all conspire to make a life.

In ancient times, the 12th house was sometimes called the house of suffering, or the "call to the monastery." Today we could say that having an astrological 12th house emphasis calls you to serve the collective spiritually or psychologically; and that not being conscious of *that world* might cause you suffering.

చ్‌ఄ

So, North Node *medicine* is about many things, but primarily it's about the effort to make conscious what is unconscious, and using that awareness to heal your self. The previous example was easy to understand because the example was simplified in that Leo and the 5th house are similar, as are Pisces and the 12th house. However, for most of us, we'll have Nodal signs and houses that aren't matched, so we have to do the work of overlapping the meanings and connotations of each. So you might have a Leo North Node, but it's in the 10th house of career instead of the 5th house of self-expression. Or that Pisces North Node falls in the 7th house of relationships, instead of the 12th house of the deep psyche.

Any beginning astrology book will give you simple meanings for the houses, but I suggest you use instead the *amplified versions* here of the signs and houses as you "track your karmic journey by sign and house." But you'll still have to do the alchemical work Of combining the two! It's as if you are being asked to rationally "grok" the two fundamental clues of sign and house, and then to take the intuitive leap to see how they fit together into the story of your life. You'll need to actively use your imagination here to combine your life story and all its particulars, with the symbolic stories and examples presented here.

✥

North Node medicine includes the psychological law of compensation, which Carl Jung thought to be one of the truest functions in the psyche. He wrote that the psyche has a natural balancing mechanism that "compensates" for itself unconsciously.

This compensation, however, can often feel quite uncomfortable, showing up as an aching back, insomnia, bad dreams, and difficulties in relationships. The compensatory function wants to maintain "homeostasis" and correct what is out of balance. This is compensatory function is what is *held* in the North Node, and is a way of describing the particular "vitamin" or anti-biotic that is just right for you in this life now. It's the particular area to which you need to bring some compensatory behavior, for example, too much righteousness? The medicine would be a little naughtiness. Too much seriousness? A little humor might be called for.

Because the Nodes are a polarity, it's important to remember that polarization calls for balance and integration. The compensating medicine always calls you to become more *whole*, not *good*. We need the highest expression of *both* Nodes, but we need the North a little bit more because of its compensating effects. The Vedic Indian tradition describes it by saying that we feed ourselves through our North Node and we can feed others through our South Node. Westerners, such as Carl Jung, talked about it in terms of *compensation*, and said that compensation was the truest natural law in the psyche! *Meaning that all nature seeks balance, and that if we don't do it consciously, the unconscious will do it for us.* Neurosis, and distorted or repressed behaviors, will tend to leak out of us when we are not maintaining a natural balance within. So...the right medicine at the right time is what we are aiming for here.

Good medicine is what happens when synchronicity is felt—when what you see in your chart and what you know of your life are congruent; synchronized, and reveal a pattern. Astrology is not meant to merely define, predict, or forecast—it's meant to stimulate our insight and make us whisper: "Ah-hah!" It's here to help us do what the oracle at Delphi commanded—"Know Thyself." Magic and mystery arise when synchronicity is felt—and when we make better choices we get a glimpse of who we really are, where we've been, and where we're going. And surrounding it all is the mystery of free will, character and fate: "the magic of the heavens above us, and the stars within us."

や め

Chapter 12
Where's my North Node? The Chart.

"We are born at a given moment in a given place and like vintage years of wine we have the qualities of the year and of the season in which we are born." C.G. Jung

Simply find your birthday below and you'll see the sign of your North Node. The descriptions and examples for each sign are in the following chapters and *automatically includes the South Node sign*. The North and South Nodes are always 180 degrees away, and therefore are always polar opposites to each other.

ॐ✍

What's a house? The chart is divided into 12 sections, called "houses" each relating to a different sphere of activity in your life. The house description of the Nodes always tells us *in what area of your life* something is happening, and where attention is needed to be paid. We are advised to move towards the area of life ruled by the house that holds the North Node, and away from the limitations of the area of the house that holds the South Node. You'll find out how to find where your house is in the chapter on *Tracking Your Karmic Journey by House*.

However, remember that it is a *polar axis* we're describing and the opposing signs and houses always have elements in common with each other. If you use **the high expression** of the South Node house and sign, you are doing well. And when you reach for the high expression of the North Node house, **you are stretching beyond your comfort zone** to maximize all you can be. That's good medicine. The sign and house that holds the North Node is an area of life that your Soul yearns to go toward, and is therefore a "great suggestion". In this section you'll see the *sign* of your North Node, and when you turn to that chapter it automatically shows the South Node. Begin there, and then go to the Houses.

Here's the North Node chart:

[Beginning day and year through last day and year: North Node Sign]
- June 7, 1913—Dec. 3, 1914: Pisces
- Dec. 4, 1914—May 31, 1916: Aquarius
- June 1, 1916—Feb. 13, 1918: Capricorn
- Feb. 14, 1918—Aug.15, 1919: Sagittarius
-

- Aug. 16, 1919—Feb. 7, 1921: Scorpio
- Feb. 8, 1921—Aug. 23, 1922: Libra
- Aug. 24, 1922—Apr. 23, 1924: Virgo
- Apr. 24, 1924—Oct. 26, 1925: Leo
- Oct. 27, 1925—Apr.16, 1927: Cancer
- Apr.17, 1927—Dec. 28, 1928: Gemini
- Dec. 29, 1928—July 7, 1930: Taurus
- July 8, 1930—Dec. 28, 1931: Aries
- Dec .29, 1931—June 24, 1933: Pisces
- June 25, 1933—Mar. 8, 1935: Aquarius
- Mar. 9, 1935—Sept. 14, 1936: Capricorn
- Sept.15, 1936—Mar. 3, 1938: Sagittarius
- Mar. 4, 1938—Sept. 12, 1939: Scorpio
- Sept.13, 1939—May 24, 1941: Libra
- May 25, 1941—Nov. 21, 1942: Virgo
- Nov. 22, 1942—May 11, 1944: Leo
- May 12, 1944—Dec. 13, 1945: Cancer
- Dec. 14, 1945—Aug. 2, 1947: Gemini
- Aug. 3, 1947—Jan. 26, 1949: Taurus
- Jan. 27, 1949—July 26, 1950: Aries
- July 27, 1950—Mar. 28, 1952: Pisces
- Mar. 29, 1952—Oct. 9, 1953: Aquarius
- Oct. 10, 1953—Apr. 2, 1955: Capricorn
- Apr. 3, 1955—Oct. 4, 1956: Sagittarius
- Oct. 5, 1956—June 16, 1958: Scorpio
- June 17, 1958—Dec.15, 1959: Libra
- Dec. 16, 1959—June 10, 1961: Virgo
- June 11, 1961—Dec. 23, 1962: Leo
- Dec. 24, 1962—Aug. 25, 1964: Cancer

- Aug. 26, 1964—Feb. 19, 1966: Gemini
- Feb. 20, 1966—Aug. 19, 1967: Taurus
- Aug. 20, 1967—Apr.19, 1969: Aries
- Apr. 20, 1969—Nov. 2, 1970: Pisces
- Nov. 3, 1970—Apr. 27, 1972: Aquarius
- Apr. 28, 1972—Oct. 27, 1973: Capricorn
- Oct. 28, 1973—July 10, 1975: Sagittarius
- July 11, 1975—Jan. 7, 1977: Scorpio
- Jan. 8, 1977—July 5, 1978: Libra
- July 6, 1978—Jan. 12, 1980: Virgo
- Jan.13, 1980—Sept. 24, 1981: Leo
- Sept. 25, 1981—Mar.16, 1983: Cancer
- Mar.17.1983—Sept.11, 1984: Gemini
- Sept.12, 1984—Apr. 6, 1986: Taurus
- Apr. 7, 1986—Dec. 2, 1987: Aries
- Dec. 3, 1987—May 22, 1989: Pisces
- May 23, 1989—Nov. 8, 1990: Aquarius
- Nov.19, 1990—Aug. 1, 1992: Capricorn
- Aug. 2, 1992—Feb. 1, 1994: Sagittarius
- Feb .2, 1994—Jul. 31, 1995: Scorpio
- Aug.1, 1995—Jan. 25, 1997: Libra
- Jan. 26, 1997—Oct. 20, 1998: Virgo
- Oct. 21, 1998—Apr. 9, 2000: Leo
- Apr.10, 2000—Oct. 12, 2001: Cancer
- Oct. 13, 2001—Apr. 13, 2003: Gemini
- Apr. 14, 2003—Dec. 25, 2004: Taurus
- Dec. 26, 2004—June 21, 2006: Aries
- June 22, 2006—Dec.18, 2007: Pisces
- Dec. 19, 2007—Aug. 22, 2009: Aquarius

Chapter 13.

Tracking Your Karmic Journey by Sign: Aries North Node, Libra South Node

Your Aries North Node Soul wants to find its courage. It wants to be excited, to explore, and even to be stressed out—- if that's what it will take to bring forth the independent and courageous side of you! Courage is the high road for Aries, and it's what we do each time we step up the plate and "show up" whether we feel like it or not. Courage is what we need to have to survive and to be a pioneer. You are the natural survivor, pioneer, entrepreneur and sacred warrior of the zodiac.

Is it that fools rush in where angels fear to tread? Or simply that your enthusiasm and fresh attitude of "why not?" motivates the rest of us? You may not feel like the fearless one—for courage is often stressed into a person by acts of bravery, but remember that courage is something you learn as you allow yourself to feel the fear and do it anyway. Your Soul may have chosen to be born into situations that have motivated you to develop the spiritual muscle of bravery. You are here to walk your talk and to learn to "step up to the plate."

As you exercise your independent nature, rather than re-enacting old tendencies of enmeshment or co-dependence, you inspire us to want to be with you, and to hear your stories, your truth. Don't be too cautious. Earlier in this life, or in former lives, you may have heeded too closely to rules of justice, reason, and skill-fully "getting along" and in the process compromised parts of yourself in a deadening attempt to please and accommodate. Now you are called to let conventional roles and habits give way to a more exciting, truthful, and passionate nature. As you dare to follow through on what truly excites your curiosities, you leave behind your South Node traces of dependency and—dare we call it "normalcy?" In this life, you don't want linger too long in any social group, for your Soul needs some alone time as well as a good dose of adventure and risk taking. Inter-dependence rather than co-dependence seems to be called for now.

For you there is a yearning for the adrenaline rush of new beginnings, and you excel at seeing fresh possibilities and new ideas. Give yourself permission not to have to follow through on every last detail. And, if you try to be overly accommodating and to try to make peace at any cost, you may lose your focus or energy. Like in the old fairytale about the Emperor who rode through the streets naked and didn't know it, *you* are meant to be the one to tell the Emperor he has no clothes on! And there's no social niceties with that one.

Aries North Node understands the paradoxical nature of people and life, and has a keen intelligence and humor that often surprises people. When you dare to act and speak outside the norm, you can delve surprisingly deep. And as a "slayer of dragons and a rescuer of maidens" (or lads) you are best when you are not only a thinker, but a doer as well....maybe even a sacred warrior.

Somewhere in the midst of your life journey, usually after your first Saturn Return (at approximately age 29) you are able to turn on your path to redeem the gold in the shadow of your Libra South Node. Redeeming the gold in the shadow of the South Node is about reclaiming your natural gifts. But these natural abilities are also your familiar path of least resistance and are best redeemed only after you have done the work of the North Node—after you have survived the slings and arrows of this new call to a courageous life. Then you can be the tactful mediator and peacemaker. Aries and Libra are ruled by Mars and Venus, respectively, and there's nothing juicier than to allow the masculine and feminine aspects of your nature to stimulate and balance each other.

Soul Purpose: Courage, survival, entrepreneurial pioneering in any field. Dependence on your own skills and abilities, rather than enmeshment with others.

Shadow: Compromising behavior and fearing to share your deepest feelings, ideas, and talents. "Going along with things" leads you into the shadows.

*** Psychological ground-breakers *Sigmund Freud and Carl Jung* both had the Aries North Node. Each of these men embodied the Aries pioneering spirit that broke new ground in the world of psychology. With South Nodes in Libra, they were called to break away from the limitations of partnerships and relationships—even with each other—and to reach for the self-directed, independent qualities of Aries.

Jung's North Node was in the 2nd house of self-worth, suggesting how important it was for him to produce a body of work that would prove himself to himself. With his South Node in the 8th house of other people's values, he needed to let go of the approval of others, and acquire the self-confidence one gets by defining oneself in one's own terms. Jung's break with Freud at his Uranus Opposition (around age forty) was extremely traumatic for Jung and precipitated his short but intense psychological breakdown. In later years, Jung's independence and disregard for other's opinions, allowed him to have intimate relationships with many people, and to explore the taboo subjects of alchemy and astrology.

Freud's North Node Aries was in the 6th house, suggesting that he was called to be both devoted to his work and to the needs of his physical body. Whether he was a hypochondriac or in as much physical pain as he said he was, was not as important as the need he had to attend to his body as well as his Work. Many people would say Freud had psychosomatic illnesses and a cocaine addiction, yet despite this, few people would discount the great work that he pioneered in his life. It's worthwhile to remember that we should never be too judgmental about another person's success or lack of success in reaching their North Node aspirations. We all fail and succeed in varying degrees.

Taurus North Node-Scorpio South Node

With your North Node in Taurus, your Soul craves peace and serenity in this life—as well as good music, a loyal lover, and picnics on the beach with good food and wine! Doesn't everybody? Yes, but not like you—-you need these things to remind your Soul that life can be good and safe and beautiful.

Having suffered too much drama and trauma either earlier in this life, or in a previous one, you're suffering now from a slight despair of spirit—one could even say that this Nodal combination has a "forgotten emotional memory" of life at its most tragic. The cure for this soul sickness is to nurture your self with the things that make life worth living. Cultivating loyal friends, enjoying nature and the physical world, and creating a beautiful home that feels like a safe harbor are all good things for you to do.

By choosing to find the "sacred in the commonplace" you re-awaken your Soul to the Divine in all things. You're not being a materialist when you truly enjoy the beauty of a hand-made wooden spoon or pottery bowl, or take time away from your work and ambitions to watch the sun set with an old friend. By seeing into the true nature of things, you get a sense of what many of the mystics have seen—that God is here and now, and found in the ordinary/extraordinary things of this life.

What do you truly value? What do you stand for in life? Something in you needs to know yourself deeper and to prove yourself worthy. The old path or habits that need to be left behind involve too much immersion in other people's dramas...a helping hand is fine, but don't get embroiled in dramas that aren't yours. Power and control issues as well as your ability to manipulate situations need to be let go of. You've done too much of that in the past. The focus now needs to be on you, and finding what you value and what nurtures you.

This life is about finding that mystical sense of belonging to a Universe that is benevolent. No easy task! It's a profound spiritual calling to find spirit in matter, and to find yourself in "right relationship" with others.

On the Taurus-Scorpio path it's important to ground yourself with a workable level of financial and emotional stability. If you can do that you're ready to retrieve the gold in the shadow—your Scorpio South Node. There's hidden wisdom and power there, for in your Scorpio past you deeply understood other people and had a keen intuitive-psychic nature. You might have been the detective, the shaman, the priest, or the power behind the throne—-the one who could hone in on the emotional bottom line. Now if you can bring your new level of security and grounded faith in the goodness of life into your relationships with others and into your work, you can nourish others with your profound wisdom.

Soul Purpose: serenity and stability, regaining a sense of the sacred in the ordinary, a sense of having earned and gained by one's own efforts, honoring good traditions and preserving what is valuable for future generations.

Shadow: Looking to another for definition, self-confidence, or too much support. Taking things that aren't yours. Collapsing into a felt sense of emotional pain from previous lives, and adapting an overly serious, gloomy attitude. Going to quickly into studying the occult and transpersonal realities, and thereby taking a spiritual bypass on your emotional life.

∂∞∞

Oscar Wilde, Irish playwright, poet, novelist, and great wit had his North Node in Taurus in the ninth house. A man who celebrated his homosexuality in Victorian England, he paid the price of his passion and suffered a dramatic downfall—he was imprisoned for it and died at the age of forty-six. Wilde certainly shows the polarity of the Nodes in his life and art, and although the Venus ruled Taurus North Node would seek serenity, he profited in the world through using his dramatic Scorpio nature. The nodes, on the 3rd/9th

house axis, relate to communication in all its forms, and his North Node in the Ninth house reflected his enthusiasm, his liberal open-mindedness, plus his enjoyment of startling people and breaking up the normality of life—all Jupiter/Sagittarius/9th house qualities. Wilde was also known for his humor and philosophic spirit—again, a 9th house trait. Although one might hope for a better balance with this polarity, and therefore a longer life for Wilde, he nevertheless might not have achieved his greatness without his life of extremes.

Gemini North Node, South Node Sagittarius

"Thou shall not tell too much Truth" was once said to a friend of mine with this Nodal combination. She was told this as a child and then it reappeared later in her life as a repeating dilemma. When she told her Truth, and lived her life by her Truth, she often got "slammed by the Universe". What was wrong?

After some discussion, she was the one who retrieved the answer. In telling her story, her opinion, her "Truth" in the Sagittarian South Node manner, she spoke it reactively, without reflection, and the abruptness of it often hurt people. Sagittarius suffers at times from "foot in mouth" disease, but more seriously, she realized that by adding more tactfulness as well as by being more objective and "contained," she could still live and speak her Truth, but in a way that didn't injure herself or others. She realized that this reflection and containment allowed her to see how life was much more differentiated into many shades of gray, rather than the black and white of her first reactive perception. This Nodal axis takes the raw experiences of life and puts them into a crucible that produces either wisdom or bitterness. By the reflective "cooking" of these Nodes, the raw anger and bitter injustices of life can be distilled, and transmuted into a compassionate wisdom.

Gemini needs new experiences. A good idea for North Node Gemini is in the motto: "Let's do something different!" Your Soul longs for new experiences and different perspectives, and you may not even know it. You may think you've seen and done it all before....but now it's time to do it differently. Earlier in this life, or in a former life, you earnestly pursued Truth and developed a powerful self-convincing story of how Reality is. However it wasn't the whole Truth; you got the view from the mountaintop perhaps, but not from the valley or the marketplace. You may have been a cloistered monk, nun, or an opinionated scholar in a former life, but it was lonely, and now it's time to ride into the market-place and take a fresh look at things.

Indulging your curiosities and breaking up your routines are good things for you now. Go to the bookstore, the cafe, get on the internet, and find new stories to tell. In this life you are challenged to be non-judgmental, to widen your perspectives, and to really listen to another person's truth in order to cultivate empathy and open-minded thinking. Your perceptual bias is changing, so that you can see things from many different angles—not an easy thing to do! Your reality may feel shattered at times, and you may wonder where your self-confidence has gone. Certain aspects of your life need to *de-construct* so it can be *re-constructed* in a new way. . By allowing yourself to follow your dreams and gently releasing old concepts of how it all is, you begin to break new ground.

Life is breaking you open to enlarge your heart and widen your perspective; for you are being trained to be the compassionate communicator. You can be the one with new stories to tell that are grounded in personal experience. You're not just the book-smart armchair philosopher any more—you've walked your talk.

It will continue to be important for you to find ways to slow down, and simply connect with others in a way in which you each share the paradoxes and mysteries of life as well as your own "truths." That truth you came into this life with is in the process of getting much bigger. And as you do this, you'll find that writing, teaching, selling, counseling, and communicating in all forms can bring you great success. With your South Node in philosophic Sagittarius you've got some spiritual gold in your past, and now the trick is to take your old wisdom and new found "Gemini street smarts" and unite them. The world needs to hear what you have to say, that is, as long as you're following a path with heart.

Keep checking in with yourself that your objectivity hasn't run away with your Soul. In your desire to embrace change, be gentle towards those who lead more mundane lives and don't be too quick to judge. You have so much to give!

Soul Purpose: It's important for you to immerse yourself in the fullness and chaos of life; indulging your curiosities, being a communicator, and daring to risk your security for a life of adventure, both inner and outer. In telling your Truth and your stories skillfully, with objectivity and reflection, you awaken others to great insight. Communication is a key, but communication is not limited to words alone; it is inherent in the arts, healing practices, and in the "act of loving" in relationships.

Shadow: Your default pattern of letting your enthusiasm override your empathic listening, combined with a philosophic "know it all" attitude, could blind you to life's complexities and wonders. If you are addicted to certainty, you will deny truths or experiences that run counter to your expectations and belief. Allow room for dialog and relationships that challenge you to expand your concepts of "how it all is."

ক্ক

Maya Angelou, much loved American sage, writer, artist and civil rights activist has a Gemini North Node in the 10th house of career and public life. She has been called "America's most visible black female autobiographer". Angelou is known for her series of six autobiographies, starting with *I Know Why the Caged Bird Sings in* 1969. She has been telling her story! Her volume of poetry, *Just Give Me a Cool Drink of Water 'Fore I Diiie* (1971) was nominated for the Pulitzer Prize. As testimony to her success, Angelou recited her poem, "On the Pulse of Morning" at President Bill Clinton's inauguration.

Emerging from a violent and emotionally impoverished childhood, her South Node in Sagittarius in the 4th house expressed itself through harsh experiences of poverty and abuse, yet she was able to *skillfully* find a way to speak her truth with reflection and empathy through her writing and lecturing.

"*I Know Why The Caged Bird Sings*" represents Angelou's experience of racism and other forms of potential imprisonment: by drugs, marriage, or the economic system. This metaphor of the bird in the cage invokes the "supposed contradiction of the bird singing in the midst of its struggle". Maya communicates constantly (Gemini) the necessity for people to arise above conflict and despair, and to embrace life with renewed (Sagittarian) enthusiasm despite the circumstances.

Maya has used her Gemini survival skills and street smarts to rise above a childhood that could have imprisoned her—and as she says in one of her autobiographies: "Women who survive must be at once both tender and tough." This combination of tender empathy, reflective thinking, and an intense desire to communicate expresses the essence of this Nodal axis.

Maya's most common speaking engagements occur on college campuses, "where seating is sold out
long before the actual event." When Angelou speaks,
she sits on a stool and entertains the audience for approximately one hour, reciting poems by memory
and following a flexible outline. Entertaining people,
whether through poetry, music or acting, is a form of
communication that reaches across boundaries and
prejudice. Maya has been a public charismatic figure
for most of her life, and is one of the world's great wise
women.

Cancer North Node, South Node Capricorn

When you work a long day, its good to come home and rest, and when you feel the need for help, its good to feel comfortable enough to ask for it. But for you, there can be a resistance to these very natural things. Somewhere in your past, either earlier in this life or in a previous one, you've worked hard pursuing your goals and doing what needed to be done. You've come into this life with an attitude that knows how to survive by being practical and by adapting to the harsh realities of life and making a living. (Some of you have even allowed an almost pathological sense of caution or reserve to develop in response to having to keep a stiff upper lip.) Now it's time to soften, relax, and heal from being in a competitive and overly pressured environment.

Now it's time to shift focus from "them to you", and to take the emphasis off the goal and onto the process of life unfolding. How do you *feel* about what's happening? That's the question to consider. Part of your soul purpose is to heal from the limitations of your past, so there's a necessity at times, to cry a few tears...to simply feel. It's not giving into self—pity though, and you won't linger long in that place, for the balanced attitude of your Capricorn/Cancer axis is one that innately knows how to hold the tension of the opposites.

After your first Saturn return around the age of 29 the emphasis will turn even more towards nurturing yourself, your family, and your friends. Home, heart, and hearth become a priority. There's a desire to feel secure and at home with those you love. You may want to feel a kind of "heart security" you may never have experienced before.

In the past you may have had times when you've had to shut yourself down emotionally, and now you realize you've missed something in the focusing on the goal rather than the process. Some of the sweetness and joy of life won't happen if you're focused on goals and ambition rather than taking the time to tend to your inner life.

Cancer North Nodes are nurtured by being by the ocean (or any bodies of water) by delving into their family history, and by honoring the good part of traditions. The family karmic inheritance is usually strong, and it would be good for you to sift through the positive and negative inheritance you've received and to see what part of it you may be unaware of.

Cancer, being ruled by the moon, fluctuates in its moods and has a wild and loony side as well. No other sign can be so content cleaning out its closets one moment and dancing on the beach by the light of the moon later the same day. With your North Node here you'll want to honor this intuitive and lunar side of yourself because it's the fertile soil of your Soul. Take time to slow down and feel whatever comes up for you, and when you feel you've outgrown your current life, dare to let go of the past and open a new chapter of your life. Cancers, like the crab, periodically outgrow their shells and need to bravely release their fears and defenses to bring new dreams into reality. The pull of continued growth and evolution through regeneration and resurrection is strong in this Cancer/Capricorn axis.

Soul Purpose: In this life it's important for you to heal from duty and necessity—you may need to cry a few tears to unblock your emotions and express your true feelings. You may also want to make it a priority to give and receive love, and to watch what happens when you tend to the process of life rather than the goal. Dare to risk new beginnings that lead to metaphorical death, re-birth and resurrection, taking calculated risks. Use your sense of humor to repair, entertain, and mend bridges between family and friends.

Shadow: Honoring of the demands of "sheer practicality" can be an excuse to not be in touch with your feelings of sorrow or joy. By not allowing the feminine and "lunar or looney" side of your personality out, it can make you appear to be a bit of a glum "Eeyore" at times. Another defense mechanism you might be tempted to use could simply be an appearance of pride—the kind of "Hubris that cometh be-fore a fall."

કેન્જ

English blues rock guitarist, singer/songwriter **Eric Clapton** has these Cancer/Capricorn Nodes. Often viewed today by critics as the greatest guitar-ist of all time, his music—and life—has always been grounded in the blues. When Eric was 9 years old he discovered that he and his brother had been deserted by his real parents, and that they'd been raised by his grandparents. When his brother died unexpectedly, Clapton became, in his own words, "a lonely and nas-ty kid." (Maybe just an Eeyore?) He tried playing the guitar but found it so difficult to learn that he almost gave up, but the connection to his emotions through the "blues" pulled him through and kept him at it. So instead of shutting down his feelings or being out of touch with them, as South Node Capricorns can do at times, he reached for them—through 'the blues." One of his more famous songs in his later life was called: "Tears in Heaven," that came out of the unexpected tragic death of his son.

Before this, at one point in mid-life, Clapton let his emotions slip into serious drug abuse, but with help he was able to get clean and later opened a drug rehabilitation clinic which he still financially sup-ports. Clapton has mixed the professional Saturnian hard working nature of Capricorn with his fluctuating emotional life to make a powerful impact in the world of music. He uses his music to connect deeply with the promptings of his heart, and in healing himself, he heals all of us.

Leo North Node, South Node Aquarius

It's time to take center stage! Have you been waiting for the support of friends or colleagues, or even for "more information" before stepping up to the plate in your life? Your Soul yearns to come forward now, to take chances, to see life as a game worth playing—simply because it's fun and a challenge. Somewhere in your past you may have lost a joyful sense of play and spontaneity and now it's time to recover your exuberant self-confidence, and to share it.

Either earlier in this life or in a former life, you were living on the sidelines watching others interact on center stage. You felt exiled, even if you weren't. Now its time to engage yourself actively—be creative with a paintbrush, your children, or simply with how you live each day. Color outside the lines of your everyday life and rejoice at the results. "Follow your bliss" the mythologist Joseph Campbell was fond of saying, and as the Persian poet, Rumi once said: "Let the beauty you love be what you do. There are a thousand ways to kneel and kiss the earth." Following your passion is good North Node medicine for you. If you don't know what "your bliss" is, then you are called to listen to yourself more—ask yourself: what makes you laugh, cry, rage?

When a person holds the energies of the rebel, the genius and the outsider, we see the signature of

Aquarius strong in the chart—often with a South Node in Aquarius. There's an unconscious soul conditioning here to think differently, and therefore you may be aware of not being really heard. You may speak your Truth, but not understand how it's being received. So learning to communicate well, and with empathic feeling is important for you. A person with a South Node Aquarius can tend to be so objective or so focused in one direction, that he loses touch with the feeling based world he lives in.

Why is this? In re-incarnationally based evolutionary astrology. it could be said that you may have soul-memories of persecution or even torture, so there can be a tendency to dissociate at times—a reflex defense that "gets you away emotionally". And why not, if you might have suffered as an exiled heretic before? Now, you are moving away from that lonely position of being the outsider to the savvy position of being effective in the world—and feeling connected to others. You are learning to love and to express yourself with others who might have burned you at the stake in a former life for the beliefs you held. Whew—evolutionary re-incarnational theory can get intense at times.

So...whether married or single, don't detach yourself from emotional situations, but engage yourself fully and find ways to keep all your relationships fresh and alive. But this is not a license for irresponsibility, in fact, you may be surprised by how upset people can get with you when you act carelessly around issues of trust or with changing plans—people can get quite attached to you and take your actions too personally. It is also through the interrelationship with others that you'll find the high energy and passion that feeds you.

In this life it's healing for you to leave behind an overly balanced sense of objectivity, seriousness, and perhaps aloofness as well. You are meant to open your generous heart to everyone this time around and to let your true light shine. Be real and unique, for you have the soul of a performer, the touch of the aristocrat, and the charm of a child. You've come into this life to be seen and accepted and to feel the joy of knowing love. Dare to give your talents and gifts to the world. Don't wait for others to ask you—take the initiative yourself.

As you turn on your path and retrieve the gold in the shadow of your South Node of Aquarius, you may find that you have a talent for discovering fresh ideas, new inventions, and innovative ways of being in the world. However be mindful of what groups and friends you choose to affiliate yourself with. There is a tendency for some N. Node Leos to get into groups they don't have a natural affinity with. When you act from your own passions, values, and priorities you'll naturally find the people who are right for you. Don't sacrifice who you really are for the appearance of popularity or for the sake of duty. Instead, keep your mind on your intuitive promptings and proceed step by step to making your dreams a reality...and in the process you'll find your true friends as well.

Soul Purpose: To create loving connections with others in order to heal the sense of being the outsider or the persecuted one. By leaving behind harsh judgments of self or others, the idea now is to "Come in from the cold and become one of us." Join with the family of man, and make your presence felt. Be effective and compelling rather than "being right" and alone.

Shadow: A deeply entrenched unconscious fear can entice you to be controlling, inflexible or stubborn especially in the little things of life. Practice forgiveness and letting your funny bone out. You could be a good comedian! Humor acknowledges the dark side of life with a detached and ironic perspective. A heartfelt humor that knows the pain of life can accept the full drama of it as well.

∂∾⋖

Folk/rock singer songwriter Joni Mitchell has this Nodal combination. Writer of songs such as "Woodstock" and "Both Sides Now" Joni has had great professional and personal success in her life. As a child, Joni moved around Canada quite a bit with her parents, but discovered her passion and joy at an early age: At the age of nine, Mitchell contracted polio during a Canadian epidemic, but she recovered after a stay in hospital. It was during this time that she first became interested in singing. She describes her first experience singing while in hospital during the winter in the following way: "They said I might not walk again, and that I would not be able to go home for Christmas. I wouldn't go for it. So I started to sing Christmas carols and I used to sing them real loud... The boy in the bed next to me, used to complain. And I discovered I was a ham."

In later life, Joni was able to happily reunite with her daughter whom she had given up for adoption earlier. Her early life feelings of social disconnection (past life?) could be described in an interview she gave to the *The New York Times* in which she said that her memoirs were "in the works", and that the first line would be "I was the only black man at the party."

Virgo North Node, South Node Pisces

Virgo is probably the least understood and most under-estimated sign of the zodiac.

Whether it is your Sun sign or your North Node sign, you have a unique ability to visualize the ideal and the willingness to do what must be done to bring this ideal into reality. What a gift! However for you to do the high path of Virgo, you must use the tools of discrimination and discernment—which also means you need to "dot your i's and cross your t's." By carefully attending to the little details of life, and by analyzing what's really happening, you'll be able to make your dreams come true.

Earlier in this life, or in a former life, you've merged with the Divine in some way and yet you weren't savvy about how to live the mundane life on earth. Whether you merged with God, your Art, your lover, or your bottle of wine, you now need to relax the urge to merge and pay attention to the demands of reality. Some of you may have died, suffered, or been persecuted because of your beliefs, so now you need to regain your faith that life in the real world can be good. Many lifetimes may have been spent in the dissolution or sacrifice of ego or simply sacrificing your life for the sake of another person or ideal. Now it's time to develop a healthy ego and strong sense of Self that allows your Soul to feel safe.

As a North Node Virgo, you've been naturally drawn towards developing a vision of the "ideal" and you innately know how to bring that vision into reality. Don't allow yourself to get distracted, but get good at the mundane details of life and see how that process of focusing and becoming competent enables you to bring your dreams into reality.

Dare to take risks in spite of fears, and avoid addictive tendencies and escapism. The wisdom and sense of Oneness you earned in former lives can now support you in this world. Because you see the ideal and are willing to work for it, you often get what you want, as long as you don't let your perfectionism or self-criticism stop you from giving 100 percent in whatever you do. There is a need to plan and strategize in this life and follow through on your ideas.

You are likely to have skills in crafts, teaching and in the healing professions, but whatever you do, use skillful means to your ends, and empowerment will happen naturally. You have a psychic sensitivity, a great imagination and a uniquely creative way of seeing things. These attributes, plus an innate understanding of people helps you in countless ways.

As you turn on your path and retrieve the gold in the shadow of Pisces, remember your half-forgotten visions and sense of knowingness..."remember to remember" all that is good and beautiful and meaningful in life. Remember the magic you know in your heart.

Soul Purpose: to bring order, harmony, healing, and practical wisdom into your life and the lives of those you touch. By knowing what is truly good—since you've been doing the work of "separating the wheat from the chaff" and the real from the illusory, you preserve and maintain the best of what our culture and our mutual lives have to offer. Learn a skill and offer it to the world. When you become truly useful to others—when you are "in service" to others—you regain a lost sense of self and self-appreciation.

Shadow: A default tendency to see the world as a dream, and one in which you don't have a strong sense of Self. You may have spent lifetimes dissolving the ego in unselfish tasks, or religious life, but that stance doesn't serve you now. In a former life you may not have developed a strong enough ego that could have helped you thrive—you might not have been "mirrored well" as a child, or you may have lost your sense of sense in the collective (like in the military) or in addictions (communing with the bottle.) When you don't look beyond your inner world to skillfully participating in life, you sink into a dull dream of life that's bound by other people's expectations, and you lose that cherished love that comes from serving and loving others. There's a subtle difference here—basically, give your gift/service to the world, but do it your way!

&ost;&osc;

Joseph Campbell had this Virgo/Pisces Nodal polarity. Campbell was a world famous mythologist, writer, and lecturer in comparative religion and mythology who also became popular to the American public due to the PBS television series, the" Power of Myth" with Bill Moyers. In this series, Americans remember him for his depth of sharing on the "myth of the hero" through all cultures, the Universality of certain spiritual "truths" and the necessity for "following one's bliss" in life.

As a North Node Virgo, Campbell tackled the enormous job of chronicling, cataloging and synthesizing details of the world's mythologies and religions. His painstaking analysis allowed us to see connections and parallels in man's religious nature—the kind of work that Carl Jung had also done.

However Campbell began his studies in the time of the Great Depression, and when conventional graduate school wasn't available to him he devised a plan of study as he was trying to figure out what to do with his life. He engaged in a period of intense and rigorous independent study which he discussed in The Hero's Journey: Joseph Campbell on His Life and Work. Campbell states that he "would divide the day into four four-hour periods, of which I would be reading in three of the four hour periods, and free one of them...I would get nine hours of sheer reading done a day. And this went on for five years straight." Now this is reaching for that skillful and disciplined North Node Virgo!

Campbell believed the religions of the world to be culturally influenced "masks" of the same fundamental, transcendent truths. All religions, including Christianity and Buddhism, can bring one to an elevated awareness above and beyond a dualistic conception of reality—that is, beyond the idea of "pairs of opposites," such as being and non-being, or right and wrong. Indeed, he quotes in the preface of *The Hero with a Thousand Faces* "Truth is one, the sages speak of it by many names." In this line, we can hear the echo of his Pisces South Node: that place in him that could permeate beyond boundaries, masks, and linguistic or cultural divisions.

Campbell's body of work was huge and even affected the world of screenwriting and film. George Lucas was the first Hollywood filmmaker to openly credit Campbell's influence. Lucas stated following the release of the first *Star Wars* film in 1977 that its story was shaped, in part, by ideas described in *The Hero With A Thousand Faces* . Campbell's life itself was like a film of one hero's journey, and contains both the discipline and the imagination of the Virgo/Pisces axis.

Libra North Node, South Node Aries

Achieving "serenity" is a soul aspiration for you in this lifetime, although the thrill of the hero's journey and the grand quest is strong for you with these Nodes. Your South Node is ruled by the mythical hero, Mars, who embodies the ideal of the spiritual warrior and the one who breaks new ground. However, with your North Node in Libra, ruled by Venus, it is through the more feminine side of yourself that you come *home* to yourself. Venus compensates for the excesses of Mars, and yet she can be a demanding muse or irritation, depending on how you treat the masculine/feminine polarity within yourself.

With this Nodal axis it will be important for you to find ways to calm down, release tension, and allow all forms of beauty and harmony to heal you. Like a finely turned violin, you need to catch stress and pressure before it causes something to snap. There may have been something exhausting earlier in this life or in a previous life experience where you placed great emphasis on personal achievement, self-sacrifice and courageous action. Now it's time to release the singular survival urge and ambitious mentality to develop your North Node's Soul's yearning for deep serenity. For you, this suggests nurturing co-operative relationships and finding release from the mental/emotional "tension of the opposites."

The symbol of your Venus ruled Libra North Node is the ancient image of Athena holding the Scales. This mental weighing and balancing of the 'great opposites" in life is exhausting, yet the challenge of knowing what is "right and fair and true" is too delicious not to embrace. You delight in having had the courage (South Node Aries) to go where others have not, to endure, and to bring home the "golden fleece". Yet it is ultimately about the learning of "right relationship" that is one of the main tasks for you in this life. It will require a relaxing of some old ways of thinking and being, as you create win/win situations with others and relax the urge to engage in victim-rescuer scenarios.

As your understanding of human nature grows, you acquire a tolerance for paradox and ambiguity and for the many different ways people perceive reality. As this increasing acceptance of the complexities of life and people grow you may find yourself in positions of peace-keeping or as a counselor or mediator.

You can excel in the Venusian fields of art, entertainment, and beauty, if you choose to develop this side of your nature. Home, heart, and hearth can take on increasing importance—one could say that these Venus ruled areas are good *compensatory medicine* for you. As you grow into a more balanced focus on interdependence rather than too much dependence or independence, you'll finally find a way to assert yourself with more confidence and without creating conflict.

Your compassionate objectivity can bring a deep contentment into your life and into the lives of anyone you touch.

Earlier in this life, or in a previous life, chances are that you were engaged in "a serious battle" of some sort. It could have been a war, or it may be a vague emotional memory of trauma. However, those leftover default patterns, or shadow qualities of Mars—the feeling of needing to know, to be right, and in your place of power, only increase the dramatic, intense and overly emotional backdrop of your past life that your Soul longs to move away from. Your unconscious knows the horror of trauma and drama, yet you also know how to numb the effects of battle, and how to create the soothing rush of the adrenaline high with a new beginning. You can dare to slow down. The war is over; you've won.

As you move to redeem the "gold in the shadow of Aries" in mid-life you may need to become less self-centered to find the serenity and co-operation with others you desire—and how many and varied the ways you may consciously and unconsciously do this! No matter how accommodating you may see yourself, you may occasionally need to dip back into this gold in the shadow, and tap into that Martian/Aries assertiveness again. Yes, Libra is about balance, justice and beauty, but without a good dose of the Martian courageousness and sense of adventure, Libra can be ineffective and indecisive. As you continue to learn to tolerate the complexities and paradoxes in life (an on-going Libran task!) you discover a new sense of equanimity, and you may notice that life comes to you, rather than you having to go to it. Allow yourself *time* to not rush into making decisions—you need to weigh and balance all the different ways you perceive and think about things.

In the latter part of your life you're more likely to seek the comfort of love rather than the drama of love earned through effort and ambition. Where there is no war, there is also greater beauty.

Soul Purpose: To cultivate a willingness to see all sides of a question and be able to forgive. Release the addiction to passion, ambition, and anger as personal fuel, and replace it with the Venusian nurturing qualities inherent in all things beautiful—music, nature, and art are all healing for you.

Shadow: Having to be right and to righteously defend a cause while causing a lot of inner and outer disturbance. Too much emphasis on the powers of the ego and not enough on the Self, and/or Self in relationship to others.

ᷤᷤ

William Butler Yeats, Irish poet, dramatist, astrologer and occultist, was one of the foremost figures of 20th century literature. Yeats had his North Node in Libra, South Node in Aries, and despite (or because of) his many literary accomplishments, he is often looked at curiously for his unusual love life and his passionate quest for a direct experience of Spirit. His many relationships with women were tumultuous, and the Venusian muse was particularly hard on him. He was refused in marriage multiple times by Maud Gonne, the love of his life, and again by his proposal of marriage to her daughter.

Yeats was in love with Maud Gonne for 28 years (a full Saturn cycle) and claimed to have a spiritual marriage with her—perhaps providing Yeats with the emotional suffering necessary for an alchemical breakdown to take place. It seems significant that Yeats' life long desire to channel spirit information came to him, not by the excesses of his passion, but through his later life marriage to his wife, Georgie. One cannot know if he found the "serenity" that is the hallmark for Libra, but one could hope that in accepting the responsibility of their marriage and two children, Yeats may have turned the base metal of everyday human life into the gold he so yearned for in his spiritual quest.

As a member of the occult society of the *Golden Dawn* it became necessary for Yeats to grasp the unity of opposition over and over again, and the necessity of alchemical healing through suffering and purification. His magical name in that society: *Demon Est*

Deus Inversus (the Devil is God inverted) underlines that opposition.

Yeats knew that in Vedic Indian astrology, his "head of the dragon, Rahu," was in Libra, and the "tail of the dragon, Ketu," was in Aries. C.G. Jung wrote in his book, *Mysterium Coniunctionis*."...in the image of the uroboros (the serpent or dragon swallowing its own tail) lies the thought of devouring oneself and turning oneself into a circulatory process. The uroboros is a dramatic symbol for the integration and assimilation of the opposite, i.e., of the shadow..."

It is interesting to note that the South Node *shadow* for Yeats was in Aries, with it's polar opposite, in compensatory Venus ruled Libra, while the opposite is true for two other men who pioneered in the area of the unconscious—Sigmund Freud and Carl Jung. They both had the opposite polarity of North Node being in Mars ruled Aries, and South Node in Libra. All three men shared the passionate Venus/Mars polarity with its intense interest/disinterest in sexuality, love, and the life of the spirit.

Scorpio North Node, South Node Taurus

The passionate Scorpio nature feels its way through life, sensing undercurrents and daring to look deeply to find the emotional bottom line. In order to move towards the heights of your Scorpio North Node you need to relax your concerns around money, security, and possessions as well as being willing to risk losing your current level of comfort to gain a higher state of power and vitality.

Can you leave behind tendencies to possessiveness and attachment and open up to the excitement of change? Will you dare to look deeply and bravely into the underworld, into 'the other side of the question' and into the places where the deepest level of truth resides? Superficial "people pleasing" is not for you. You are meant to look into the eyes of the murderer and find the frightened unloved child there. You are meant to know the whole story, and to travel the roads many of us declare unsafe.

The eagle, the phoenix, and the scorpion are the symbols of Scorpio, and like the eagle you were meant to fly high and be powerful, and like the phoenix, you are meant to risk dying and being reborn, knowing you are a survivor. As you dare to delve into the mysteries of life, you come up with deep treasure.

The third symbol of the scorpion hints at the shadow side of this sign which can see all aspects of truth, including that which is not always full of light and joy. The wisdom of the Scorpio nature evolves because it has dared to explore the dark, the taboo, the unspoken, and then takes this ability to see and embrace the dark and transform it. It's a high calling and that's why North Node Scorpios are often the best doctors, healers, investigators, and friends to have in times of crisis.

Scorpios are the truth-tellers of the zodiac. In the old storybook tale it was probably a Scorpio who told the emperor he had no clothes on. Because you are good at delving into the minds of others, you can be intense, yet your Soul yearns to deeply relate to others and benefits by working in partnership. Let yourself explore and experience what sex, money, God, and politics can teach you. Go where others have not, and let yourself experience it all. Be brave, for like the cat with many lives, you too have many lives to live.

When you come to a turning point in the Scorpio-Taurus path you're ready to retrieve the gold in the shadow of your Taurus South Node. You can now relax into enjoying the fruit of your passions. For example, turn the grist from the mill of your life into something creative and pleasing. Have you ever tried singing or songwriting? (Taurus rules the throat and singing.) Or writing a mystery novel or screenplay? Own your experiences by creatively giving birth to something that is uniquely you.

Soul Purpose: Integrating your instinctual goodness and vulnerability with a willingness to do the hard and often conflictual work of making both relationships and career "work" for you. You have to go deeper than you may be comfortable with, and learn to move beyond "goodness" into wholeness. This means having the ability to withdraw negative projections from others, and to see with compassion where you may have control issues, sexual hungers, and feelings that are sometimes less than nice. You are meant to make peace with you own "inner scorpion." Doing this will give you a power and charisma that will make you successful in whatever areas of life you choose to dwell in.

Shadow: Trying to keep everything safe and predictable. You are called to the edge to look at the complexities of life and the moral ambivalence and paradoxes of life. Not an easy thing to do! Being lazy and going for the creature comforts only puts you back into old habits. Release any addiction to financial security as being the "bottom line."

ॐॶॶ

Ellen DeGeneres, Emmy Award-winning stand-up comedienne, actress and host for the syndicated "The Ellen DeGeneres Show" has this Nodal combination. Although we can't know the details of her personal experience in reaching for her phoenix-like Scorpio North Node, we can see her gutsy, hard working, truth telling nature in her public expression. We know that before becoming famous, Ellen worked as a waitress, house painter, bartender, and retail clerk. And we know that she came out publicly as a lesbian in an appearance on *The Oprah Winfrey Show* .

DeGeneres received wide exposure on November 4, 2001, when she hosted the Emmy Awards-TV show. Presented after two cancellations due to network concerns that a ceremony following the September 11, 2001 attacks would appear insensitive, the show required a more somber tone that would also allow viewers to temporarily forget the tragedy. DeGeneres received several standing ovations for her performance that evening which included the line: "We're told to go on living our lives as usual, because to do otherwise is to let the terrorists win, and really, what would upset the Taliban more than a homosexual woman wearing a suit in front of a room full of Jews?"

Ellen became formally married to Portia de Rossi in 2004, and they live together as Vegans with their three dogs and four cats. As a lover of animals, and as a savvy business woman, Ellen faced a dilemma in the 2007 writer's strike when she crossed the picket line to do her television show. Although Degeneres verbally supported the strike she said that she could not break her contracts or risk her show losing its time slot. As a show of solidarity with the strikers, DeGeneres omitted her monologue during the strike, typically written by WGA writers. However, the Writer's Guild condemned her, and said that she was "not welcome in NY" saying: "We find it sad that Ellen spent an entire week crying and fighting for a dog that she gave away, yet she couldn't even stand by writers for more than one day—writers who have helped make her extremely successful."

This Taurus/Scorpio Nodal combination can sometimes put one into situations where we need to be true to ourself and our needs, as well as true to what we believe is correct. Whether we believe she was wrong or right in her decisions, I think Ellen showed courage in her stance of truth telling, both in her coming out in her sexuality/marriage, her humor-filled tactfulness after 9/11, and in her business needs—she is a good example of the complexities of choice and moral ambivalence contained in the Scorpio North Node.

Sagittarius North Node, Gemini South Node

Having come into this life with the talent for seeing so many different points of view, it's important now for you to continually hone in on your own "Truth" and find the philosophic rudder for your life. It's good for you to keep seeing life as a quest and as a profound journey in which you keep expanding and integrating your experiences. By allowing yourself freedom and time for reading, traveling, and being out in the world you acquire the experiences that nurture you.

Earlier in this life, or in a past life it was important for you to be quick, fast talking, and to know all the answers if you could. You were willing to try many things and sought to understand how others thought and acted—-but now your Soul yearns to look beyond the relativity of everything to find some essential Truth of your own to live by.

This new philosophic grounding, or rudder, allows you to see life as a grand adventure, and to feel a certain safety in your position. Your psyche, like a sailboat, won't tip so easily when your Soul has framed your experiences in a way that allows for mistakes, changes, and even betrayals, because there is a growing understanding of how human and divine nature interact. You now have the wisdom to see life as a grand adventure, and it's important to take the time to share with others what you've discovered about the meaning of life. You need to find new ways to tell your story.

There's a bit of the gypsy, scholar and philosopher in you. And as you develop your intuitive nature more and speak from your higher mind, your friends will delight in your storytelling ability and deep wisdom. You're in the process of leaving behind the impatient, overly logical part of yourself that constantly hungers for more factual information. When you spend time by yourself in nature, or pondering a reflective book, or simply open yourself up to true inspiration, you begin acquiring a deeper purpose in life and a soul-full resonance that echoes in the way you present yourself to the world.

As you move along this path, you new found sense of security in this life allows you to keep a good attitude and an optimism that attracts others. You are also good at distributing "good and fair ideas" and you would do well as a teacher or speaker in whatever field you have competence in.

As you pick up the gold in the shadow of Gemini, you treasure the wealth and variety of different experiences you've had in the past—-you've lived more in one life that some people have in many. And now you're able to pull it all together into a coherent life. The new Sagittarian vision is one that adds meaningfulness to the full palate of your Gemini experiences.

Soul Purpose: Expanded consciousness and a wide breath of experience, through study, travel or contact with other cultures, that encourages a philosophy of life that you live by, and perhaps teach. You need to give yourself time to think about the big picture of your life, to ponder what all your efforts will amount to, and then avoid the distractions that keep you from achieving your highest ideals.

Shadow: Over-extension, over-doing, and "tripping the life fantastic." Are you all about too many tactics and clever action, but have no long range strategy or goal for your life? Are you constantly avoiding commitments in order to keep your options open? Release any addiction to the desire "to stay forever young." With your keen intellect and sense of wonder and curiosity, you may have a talent with language and communication—be sure to use it soulfully and not glibly.

～◌◌

Bill Gates has this nodal polarity. As American business magnate, philanthropist, and the world's third richest person (as of February 8, 2008), he is chairman of Microsoft, the software company he co-founded. Gates is one of the best-known entrepreneurs of the personal computer revolution. Although he is admired by many people, others criticize his business tactics, which they consider anti-competitive, an opinion which has in some cases been upheld by the courts. In the later stages of his career, Gates has pursued a number of philanthropic endeavors, donating large amounts of money to various charitable organizations and scientific research programs through the Bill & Melinda Gates Foundation, established in 2000.

Before getting married, Bill's focus was strictly business oriented. From Microsoft's founding in 1975 until 2006, Gates aggressively broadened the company's range of products, and wherever Microsoft achieved a dominant position he vigorously defended it. First hand accounts of Gates in business meetings describe him as verbally combative, berating managers for perceived holes in their business strategies—he often interrupted presentations with such comments as, "That's the stupidest thing I've ever heard!"and, "Why don't you just give up your options and join the Peace Corps?"

Bill was born with Gemini street smarts, and has been known to even brag about his IQ. However street smart savvy he is, one wonders if he would have ever moved towards his philosophic Sagittarian North Node without the influence of his wife. Sagittarius is ruled by Jupiter which rules both humanitarian and philosophic endeavors, as well as all things expansive and abundant One could make a case that Gates didn't find the philosophic rudder of his ship till he married his wife, Melinda. Gates on January 1, 1994 and began a new career as the father of three children.

Bill Gates stepped down as chief executive officer of Microsoft in January, 2000. In June, 2006, Gates announced that he would be transitioning from full-time work at Microsoft to full-time work in his philanthropy foundation. One wonder perhaps if in some way he is the one who is now joining the Peace Corps? Bill and Melinda's foundation has given away over 14 *billion* dollars so far, and its estimated that Bill and Melinda will give away close to 100 billion in their lifetime. Melinda has also recently unveiled a plan to eradicate malaria, which the couple will help finance.

I suspect it was Bill's acceptance of Melinda in his life that made all the difference in his life's trajectory. It's much more comfortable for people with lots of Gemini and Sagittarius in their chart or on the Nodes, to rally around the cry "don't fence me in!" Partnership commitment, intimacy and receptivity to others on a deep level doesn't come easy for them. According to Wikipedia, friends of the couple say that Bill wouldn't be shifting gears if it weren't for Melinda. Moreover, they say, she has helped Bill become more open, patient, and compassionate. "Bullshit!" he bellows. Nicer, perhaps? "No way!" he shouts, grinning because he knows it's true. About the philanthropic work he says, "I don't think it would be fun to do on my own, and I don't think I'd do as much of it." The couple's close friend, financial wizard, Warren Buffett, who has known them since 1991 says: "Bill really needs her." However, it was Bill choice to bring her into his life—it was his Soul's choice. Buffett also has stated that Melinda makes Bill a better decision-maker. (Doesn't that Gemini South Node see almost too many possibilities? Indecision catches the Gemini South Node as a default pattern as a first response—but then once committed, Sagittarius will defend any personal cause to the bitter end....and he certainly defended Microsoft.) "He's smart as hell," Buffett went on to say. "But in terms of seeing the whole picture, she's smarter." Would Buffett have given the Gates Foundation *his fortune* if Melinda were not in the picture? "That's a great question," he replies. "And the answer is, I'm not sure."

Capricorn North Node, South Node Cancer

Integrity is the key to your life. By following your personal code of ethics and beliefs you have an inner compass for your life. As you develop self-control and self-care while approaching life in a goal oriented manner, you integrate the lessons of your past and bring your dreams into reality. In former lives, or earlier in this one, you were more concerned with the process of life rather than your goals and visions, and were overly immersed in your emotional life. At times you succumbed to moodiness and a dependence on others that was not healthy. Now you are learning to truly be the author of your life: you are coming into your own "author-ity" and finding the satisfactions of independence.

By setting positive and reachable goals, and taking the steady steps to reach them, you release old fears of rejection and find that you have what it takes to be a leader and a person in authority. This may feel quite new, as you may have spent other lifetimes in which you were a householder and identified with your role in your family and clan. You may still have some difficult family karma to resolve, but you're willing and able to do what needs to be done. You are not one to be irresponsible and you are not naive either.

In this life you are called to be a builder, a creator, and a preserver of all that is valuable. You have a deep respect for the good part of traditions that have been handed down, and you may find yourself given the opportunity to succeed in the world in a surprising way. Others see your integrity, and trust that you can be the person of authority.

Because of your innate seriousness and strong work ethic you can sometimes feel isolated from others, so make it a point to find ways to lightly and creatively express yourself, as well as finding loyal friends to cheer and encourage you. You are more respected and loved than you realize.

As you pick up the gold in your Cancer South Node, you'll find that any left-over tendencies to control others by emotional over reactions and manipulations will fall away as you come into your own. You have a keen sense of intuition and although you may feel at times as if you are blocked, or don't want to open up fully to all your emotions for fear that it is dangerous territory, you would still be wise to do so. But trust your intuitions, and go at your own pace.

Soul Purpose: Building a life, a business or career, or some structure that is worthy of your ambition. You are "toughening" into becoming an Elder and a wise one, but you need to mature into it by wise use of solitude and a savvy attitude in the world. You are leaving behind a family oriented dependence and moving out into the public world. You could become a high achiever and successful in whatever field you choose, but remember to "be in the world, but not of it."

Shadow: Not setting up appropriate boundaries between your self and family members or business partners. The goal is inter-dependence with others, and an outward looking perspective that still honors the integrity you deeply understand. Never forget the old Biblical saying: "What does it profit a man if he gains the whole world but lose his immortal Soul?"

৵৽

Oprah Winfrey, television talk show host, wise woman, and possibly one of the world's wealthiest and most influential woman, Oprah has this Nodal aspect. Born in rural Mississippi to a poor teenage single mother and later raised in an inner city Milwaukee neighborhood, Winfrey was raped at age 9, and at 14-years-old gave birth to a son, who died in infancy. She was sent to live with her father, who encouraged her education, and Winfrey landed a job in radio while still in high school. She began co-anchoring the local evening news at the age of 19. Oprah is credited with creating a more intimate confessional form of media communication, and by the mid 1990s she had reinvented her show with a focus on literature, self-improvement, and spirituality. She is generally admired for overcoming adversity and for becoming a benefactor to others—in 2006 she became an early supporter of Barack Obama, which may have helped him win the election.

Oprah shows the characteristics of deep integrity and goal orientation that is embodied in her North Node Capricorn. Her strong work ethic helped move her beyond the South Node "Cancerian immersion" in the drama of family life and she chose instead to focus her energy and goals towards the larger "family" of the world. Although Winfrey has a partner, she never married, and believes that the reason she never had children was because her students at her South Africa's Academy for Girls were meant to be her daughters: I never had children, never even thought I would have children. Now I have 152 daughters; expecting 75 more next year. I said to the mothers, the family members, the aunts, the grannies—because most of these girls have lost their families, their parents—I said: "Your daughters are now my daughters and I promise you I'm going to take care of your daughters. I promise you."

Time magazine wrote about Oprah's power to blend the public (Capricorn) and the private (Cancer): "Like a family member, it's as if she sits down to meals with us and talks to us in the lonely afternoons. She makes people care because she cares. That is Winfrey's genius, and will be her legacy, as the changes she has wrought in the talk show continue to permeate our culture and shape our lives."

Yet in 2009 Oprah has admitted that she has let her goals, ambitions and work become out of balance with her personal life and need for self-love. She admits that her life long battle with weight gain appears to be connected with a problem of self-nurturance and love, which has been a fluctuating theme in her life. This is the precarious balance of the Nodes here; balancing home, heart, and heart with the work that one is called to do. So far, it appears as if Oprah has done an amazing job of following her life direction and soul purpose.

Aquarius North Node, Leo South Node

Your soul yearns to dance to the rhythm of your own drumbeat, for in a former life or earlier in this life, you may have lived a life that had little connection to your true Self. In this life you may feel generally *liked* by your peers, as you have a charismatic "shine" about you, and others tend to project things on you which may or may not be true. They may even see you as being more lucky than you really are, or they may feel that you embody an ideal. However much others may project on you, your own true freedom and honest self-applause is more important now than the approval or praise from any group. You may have had previous lifetimes when you were on center-stage and had a fair amount of attention, and you may hold deep within you a feeling of being "special" but it may not have been a good fit for your Soul. Now there is a deep desire to be true to your self and not to follow the majority rule or herd instinct.

You care deeply about humanity and humanitarian ideas, and you need to risk disapproval from others to develop a more satisfying feeling of self approval. Because you are blessed with a keen intellect and the ability to see things differently, you have a lot to offer the world.

Aquarius North Node folks are visionaries and dreamers when they follow their North Node Soul

Path. They are astutely aware of the importance of equality and fairness, and are usually brave enough to share their ideas with others—they're the ones who write the Letters to the Editor and organize the charity fund raising and peace rallies. Known as being non-conformists, romantics, exiles and brilliant thinkers, their challenge is to inform and balance their intellects with the sometimes irrational promptings of the heart.

Yet there's always a need for greater objectivity, and a need to leave behind making changes just to exercise authority. As you learn to relate to others apart from their roles, as equals, your desire for friendship will grow. You thrive best when you nurture yourself and others with your warmth and fresh ideas.

It will be important to leave behind any old melodramatic tendencies to insist on doing things your own way, and taking dramatic risks. When you ask God and the Universe for what you want and then let it go, you allow life to bring you exactly what you need with its own perfect timing. In this life, you can relax feelings that you need to be in control and be responsible for everything.

Because Aquarius NN folks were blessed with the ability to see things that others cannot, you are challenged to bring in new ideas especially in science, metaphysics, and human rights. As an idea-breaker and visionary forerunner for the rest of us, we look to you to see where we're going.

As you turn on your path and retrieve the gold in the shadow of Leo you may want to rekindle the warmth and openness of that generous heart of yours, and then to turn that warmth and non-judgmental quality on yourself. Expect the unexpected in life and keep dancing to that distant drumbeat——life will surprise you and delight you, when you least expect it.

Soul Purpose: Being a person who knows when to preserve what is good, when to reform what is in need, and when to overthrow what is corrupt. You are called to be visionaries and dreamers who are willing to do life differently. Avoiding the seductive undercurrents of other people's expectations and projections on you is important—Aquarius is truly about freedom and authentic soul expression. Don't settle for less.

Shadow: In wanting to share your generous heart, you can come across at times as being self-centered and seeking the spotlight just a little too often. There's an awareness here of wanting to share your gift with the world, but unless you do it with a "warm touch" and pure intention it can come across at "first whiff" as being attention getting and self-serving, albeit in a rather subtle playful manner.

᚛᚜

Marianne Williamson is a spiritual activist, author, lecturer and founder of The Peace Alliance, a grass roots campaign supporting legislation currently before Congress to establish a United States Department of Peace. She has published nine books, including four *New York Times* #1 bestsellers.

A minister in the Unity Church, the driving force behind Williamson's philosophy is to offer a new thought approach to spirituality. She addresses both established Christianity and Judaism in statements such as "You've committed no sins, just mistakes." Her earliest fame came as a result of her talks in a <u>Course in Miracles</u>, a step-by-step method for choosing love over fear. She credits her breakthrough to Oprah Winfrey who invited her to the Oprah Winfrey show to discuss Williamson's first book *A Return to Love*, a book of which Oprah bought one thousand copies.

Marianne's famous poem, "Our Deepest Fear," was wrongly accredited to Nelson Mandela, but its message is unique in expressing the Aquarius/Leo Nodal axis. In this poem she challenges all of us to dare to share our light in the world—this is a good example of bringing the "shine" of the Sun ruled sign of Leo out into the humanitarian public world of Aquarius, and she does this by acknowledging the fear inherent in her own South Node of Leo.

"...Our deepest fear is not that we are inadequate. Our deepest fear is that we are powerful be-

yond measure. It is our light, not our darkness, that most frightens us. We ask ourselves, who am I to be brilliant, gorgeous, talented, fabulous? Actually, who are you not to be? You are a child of God. Your playing small doesn't serve the world. There's nothing enlightened about shrinking so that other people won't feel insecure around you. We are all meant to shine, as children do. We were born to make manifest the glory of God that is within us. It's not just in some of us; it's in everyone. And as we let our own light shine, we unconsciously give other people permission to do the same. As we're liberated from our own fear, our presence automatically liberates others."

Pisces North Node, South Node Virgo

Having been the one who was duty-bound and played according to the 'Rules' in a former life (or earlier in this one) you now have the chance to relax your linear mind and move towards your heart's true desires. What is it you truly long for now? Is it love, beauty, imaginative creativity? Or is it simply the chance to relax your guard and take in the view from the mountaintop? In the past you may have felt that you were the person who always had to do the right thing. You were being observed, and you had high expectations of yourself and others did too. You may have been a doctor, priest, or skilled craftsperson in a previous life—someone who was expected to be precise and perfect.

But now you have the chance to relax, to not be perfect and to unite the impulses of your heart with those of your head. You can dare to be gentle with yourself now, and dare to make mistakes, to let some details go, and to be as compassionate and forgiving with yourself as you are with others.

It's a good idea to practice getting out of unpleasant situations gracefully rather than being duty-bound or judgmental. You don't "have to be right" now or confrontational, and you can dare to use your intuition and take action even when you don't have all the answers. You don't have to over-analyze things any more. Part of your soul-yearning in this life is to learn to trust in the process of life and to surrender your anxieties to a higher power. You are more loved than you realize.

Pisces North Nodes often find that having two or more jobs or roles is more pleasurable than just one—-you can be an artist as well as a parent, or an accountant by day and a musician by evening. And at times you will benefit from swimming against the prevailing social currents of your time and swimming upstream like the two fish shown on the symbol for Pisces. At times you may find yourself struggling with issues around fear and faith, spirituality vs. religion or independence vs. dependence or addiction. You will find that beauty in all its forms nurtures you and helps you to access your higher power. Like the salmon that make their way home against all odds, you have the inner strength and the homing radar that can lead you to your spiritual home.

As a Pisces North Node person, you are the compassionate visionary who lights the way for the rest of us. And no matter what career path you choose, it's going to be your inner compassion and intuition that bring you success and satisfaction. As you reach for the gold in the shadow of your South Node Virgo you'll still enjoy analyzing, yet you'll be able to soften in your position—and sometimes just simply doing what needs to be done with an accepting attitude. There's a purity of heart in the Virgo ways that is released by the hopes, yearnings, and struggles of your Pisces North Node.....and remember.... that which you are reaching for, is already deep within your Soul.

Soul Purpose: Transcending boundaries by bringing compassionate and imaginative awareness into everything you do. You are meant to become an explorer of the deep psyche; the unconscious in all its manifestations, and to know that you are loved unconditionally. Let go of the idea that life "is a struggle" and embrace the idea that a pleasurable life is a good life, and that you deserve the "magic of a creative life" in which your head and heart, body and soul, work as one. The phrase "Be good to yourself" is meant for you.

Shadow: Do you still feel yourself struggling, self-doubting, and stressing about the little things in life? Lack of self-confidence, and issues around duty, guilt and shame need to be released. You are your worst enemy at those times when you buy into limiting beliefs about yourself.

৵৹

The "anti-guru Guru" J. Krishnamurti, had these Pisces/Virgo Nodes. He was raised by New Age Theosophists in the early 1900's to become a great spiritual leader, and he had enormous expectations put on him to "be right and almost beyond human" in all he did. In fact, he was expected to move into the role of becoming a World Teacher, if not "the second coming of Christ."

The pressured discipline inherent in his South Node Virgo played itself out in his early life, and ultimately brought him to a nervous breakdown/enlightenment in his late twenties. Taken out of India as a child, he was educated in England, and it wasn't until he was past his first Saturn Return in his thirties that he truly came into his Self-realization and self-confidence. At a huge assembly in Belgium, Krishnamurti stood up in front of thousands of people and declared that he was not the Messiah they were hoping for. He released himself from expectations and roles, and insisted that the only thing he could teach was how to be free. However he spoke with so much charisma, and experience bred from his personal struggles, that he created followers even in his rebellion.

Krishnamurti insisted that the only thing he could teach was about the nature of the mind itself and the way to freedom—a way that was without dogma or guidelines. He distained spiritual gurus and religions of any kind, and essentially had the heart of a mystic which shines through in his poetry. Ironically he ended up becoming just what the Theosophists predicted—a great spiritual teacher, yet what he taught was radically different than expected.

Freedom is the foundation for the Pisces North Node. Krishnamurti suffered in order to be free from limiting expectations, and he is best known for his teachings around the philosophy that: "Truth is a pathless land." The use of "spiritual imagination" is another cornerstone for Pisces, and Krishnamurti evolved into becoming a cognitive mystic who dialogued constantly about moving beyond the realms of duality that most of us live in. His teachings influenced millions of people, including metaphysicians such as David Bohm.

The Pisces North Node urges us to bring the head and the heart together, and to find ways to transcend traditional boundaries and even to flow into altered states of consciousness. Meditation, in all its forms, is one of the most time honored ways to do this, and Krishnamurti spoke endlessly about meditation—here are a few of his quotes on the subject:

> *"Meditation is one of the greatest arts in life-perhaps the greatest, and one cannot possibly learn it from anybody, that is the beauty of it. It has no technique and therefore no authority. When you learn about yourself, watch yourself, watch the way you walk, how you eat, what you say, the gossip, the hate, the jealousy-if you are aware of all that in yourself, without any choice, that is part of meditation."*
>
> *"Man, in order to escape his conflicts, has invented many forms of meditation. These have been based on desire, will, and the urge for achievement, and imply conflict and a struggle to arrive. This conscious, deliberate striving is always within the limits of a*

conditioned mind, and in this there is no freedom. All effort to meditate is the denial of meditation. Meditation is the ending of thought. It is only then that there is a different dimension which is beyond time."

Chapter 14.
Tracking Your Nodal Journey by House:

To use this section most accurately you'll need to have your birth chart and look at which of the 12 sections of the chart your Nodes fall in—remembering that the North Node looks like a set of head-phones, and the South Node looks like its reversed image: a horseshoe. (They are always exactly 180 degrees apart and retrograde.) If you don't have your chart, there are numerous sites on the internet which will show you your chart, for free, in minutes. Or if you buy this book from me directly or from my website, I include a free copy of your chart with it.

If however, you don't have your birth time—the house information won't be accurate, because it's based on the *time* of your birth

However, you can still greatly amplify your understanding of your *North Node SIGN* by reading about the HOUSE it occupies in your chart, which is the "default natural zodiac" house position if you don't have your birth time. Each description of a house will say what sign is the "undertone" for

*that position. **Reading this will add to your understanding.** Try it out—! it also offers more karmic
information that may prove surprising, interesting, and valuable to you.*

ॐ

So, to review: The house description of the Nodes
always tells us *in what area of our life* things are happening, and where attention is needed to be paid. We
are advised to move towards the area of life ruled by
the North Node, and away from the limitations of the
house that holds the South Node. However, remember that it is a polar axis we're describing, and the opposing houses always have elements in common with
each other. If you *draw attention to the areas of life
ruled by both your North and South Node house positions, than you are on the right track..* And when you
accentuate these areas of your life as being important,
then *you are stretching beyond your comfort zone* to maximize all you can be.

It is good to remember with the area of life ruled
by your South Node, that there is an emotional memory here—unconscious, but similar to a dream that we
can't quite remember—and the element of defeat and
despair remains of what we didn't get right earlier in
this life or in a former life. So be gentle with yourself
in the area of life ruled by the South Node, as this is
where you've experienced wounding before. Whether

we did it, or it was done to us, the "emotional hang-over" may feel somewhat similar.

So let's begin!

North Node in First House

Is your North Node in the first house? Then it has an undertone of Aries, and your South Node automatically falls into the 7th house, which has a Libra undertone. Add the description of the **sign** of your North Node to this **house** position to deepen your understanding of your Nodal axis:

Here, with the North Node in the First House, which has its normal ruler Aries, it reflects a soul desire towards independence and individuation—to taking care of our own needs and desires first, and putting emphasis on surviving and fighting for what we believe in. The first house is about the individual rather than the group, family or couple, so the individual needs to come first, before a healthy relationship with others can be achieved. But the house emphasis here says: pay attention to all one-on-one relationships, marriage, business partnerships, close friendships, enemies, and even close advisors, like lawyers. It is in the arena of your life that independence needs to be strongest.

At the opposite of the North Node in the first house is the South Node in the Libra ruled Seventh house of partnerships, marriage, and one-to-one relationships. We see that the default pattern which the Soul wants to leave behind involves being in relationships that are unhealthy. It points to too much en-meshment or co-dependency with another or any un-equal relationships in which you sacrifice too much.

This Libra/Aries polarity from the seventh to the first house is ultimately about the balance be-tween you and another person, between I and Thou, between Mars and Venus being in co-operative rela-tionship with each other. Even though the Nodes al-ways show an imbalance, they also show a fascinat-ing inter-relationship—and this time it's between the male and female parts of our nature. And here, it's saying that the assertive, male, independent qualities are calling to be further developed. And yet we know there is gold in the wisdom of the receptive, feeling orientation of the classically female side of ourselves. That is the "gold in the shadow." But now we need to use that assertive, goal-making part essentially Mar-tian/Aries part of ourselves to become all we can be, and not to let the emotional drama and trauma of re-lationships throw us off balance. A bit of creative ten-sion between people is a good thing when it comes to redefining who we are and what we're about, but we're never meant to lose ourselves in the other person, or to collapse in melodramatic unselfishness. (Which you could do very nobly if your partner was sick or old or.....) The goal now is to erase the fear of separation and to use a bit of enlightened selfishness to get you there. It's always easier said than done! But there is nothing healthier than a good balance of Mars and Venus: these two Nodal energies, working in the first house of the Self.

North Node in Second House

Is your North Node in the second house? Then it has an undertone of Taurus, and your South Node automatically falls into the 8th house, which has a Scorpio undertone. Add the description of the *sign* of your North Node to this *house* position to deepen your understanding of your Nodal axis:

Away with the drama and trauma and melodrama! No more tragic love stories, no more battles for power, struggles for revenge, hidden agendas and all the stuff of great novels. Just peace. Serenity. That's the movement away from the South Node in the 8th house to the North Node in the 2nd house. Your Soul needs a rest. You need to come home to yourself and to value your own resources. You are called to focus on whatever gives you emotional, financial, and physical self-confidence and freedom.

The 8th house South Node, ruled by Pluto, has struggled to transform and be re-born like the phoenix, and somewhere in all that struggling has come an exhaustion and weariness of the spirit. This life is now one where you are being called to rethink your values, your priorities, and put the Venus ruled 2nd house of Taurus back in its position of prominence. This is not the Venus of the struggle, but of gentle inquiry—-the one that has the savvy to pick her own battles and chooses the "mutual fund" that agrees with her political and ecological consciousness. This is the Venus that soothes us, and reminds us of our roots in this good earth. She'd rather write a poem than put on the dress that makes her into the femme fatale. She finds the sacred in the commonplace, and makes it extraordinary.

The South Node here has great gold in its shadowy inheritance—-it has a hard won wisdom and occult knowledge that can serve us well when used right. Certainly astrologers and those interested in astrology, have resources here in the 8th house. With this placement however, we paid too much attention to other people's business rather than our own. We were the power behind the throne, or the one who "borrowed" another's values, glory, money or husband. Our own yearning for these things seemed to make it acceptable, but we missed the basic course in ethics or fairness.

This North Node in the 2nd house is deceptively easy—-just stay away from all that occultism, and politics, and other people's money. Just be good and mind your own business. But do "mind your business" because there's a need here to prove yourself to yourself, to regain self-confidence, and to do that by creating a body of work, or to create "a life" in whatever way is meaningful to you. Does it mean creating a strong and good family? Does it mean being really good at what you do? Yes, and it also calls for you to enjoy yourself in the process, so that your Soul can remember that this Earth can be a joyful and safe place to be. You've had too much drama and trauma before, and you now need to recover from all of that. You are now meant to take pride in yourself and your accomplishments, and also to take a picnic to the beach to watch that beautiful sunset. Easy....yes?! Here's what someone wrote to my blog wrote about this placement:

"This new north node in the second house is deceptively easy" is my favorite line...ever. As a native of this nodal position, it's so amazing to be alive in an incarnation where, I, am precisely the thing which places obstacles in my way and then gets to realize that I am not bound to suffer that harsh path. I just made a huge career change thinking that I needed to go through a very difficult, rite of passage into adulthood. The necessary rite was to realize that I don't have to suffer in order to become what I am "meant" to become. Now it's time to piece back together what I can and re-establish my REAL goals." Anonymous.

North Node in Third House

Is your North Node in the 3rd house? Then it has an undertone of Gemini, and your South Node automatically falls into the 9th house, which has a Sagittarian undertone. Add the description of the *sign* of your North Node to this *house* position to deepen your understanding of your Nodal Axis:

"The breeze at dawn has secrets to tell you. Don't go back to sleep. You must ask for what you really want. Don't go back to sleep. People are going back and forth across the doorsill where the two worlds touch. The door is round and open. Don't go back to sleep." Rumi

This saying by the Persian poet, Rumi, speaks to us in many ways. With a North Node in the 3rd house you are called to learn to live with mystery, with a sense of awe, and to live with uncertainty and an open mind. To do this, you focus yourself in your daily life with great curiosity and pay attention to those around you—brothers, sisters, neighbors, everything that confronts you each day in the marketplace of life.

Rumi says: "You must ask for what you really want" and this reminds us that spiritual etiquette requires us to ask God/Universe for intervention when needed. Intention made in prayer or ritual holds a lot of weight, and it increases when we speak them to a friend over coffee in the morning. This 3rd/9th house axis stresses the importance of your communication skills in daily life, and your willingness to take your metaphysical blinders off and see what "Truth" is right in front of you.

If your South Node is in the 9th house you may be familiar with "the doorsill where the two worlds touch" if not consciously, then in the deep recesses of your psyche. Having a Ninth house South Node implies that you sought after Truth in the past—either in former lives or this one—and told yourself a self-convincing story of how it all is. You may have been a mystic or religious leader, and "right" in your own way, but you caught the view from the mountain-top, and didn't understand the view from the valley or marketplace. In some ways, you simply got it wrong. You didn't get the whole picture and your enthusiasm for an ideal or a religious or political point of view, probably undermined you in some way. Now, your ability to have an open mind to new things is a great gift to use.

So you are cautioned not to go back to sleep, (or into another state of consciousness where you only see things one way). You can do this by relaxing your ideas about needing to know all the answers. What you need now is to open up to new information and insights gained as you see the multiplicity of life and "truths" as revealed to you in the messiness of life in the "marketplace" or within family life, not the mountaintop.

You may have spent former lives in a religious organization or simply as one who distanced him/herself from the clutter and clatter of human relationships. Now you can bring some of the "gold" in the innate spiritual wisdom you had in a previous life and use it in teaching, writing, speaking and communicating to others—but this time without prejudgment or aloofness. You are ready to listen and hear the paradoxes of life now, and your curiosity, tact, and ability to convey deep truths with compassion and fresh insight is a profound gift you have to share. Use it wisely; don't go back to sleep.

North Node in the Fourth House

Is your North Node in the 4ᵗʰ house? Then it has an undertone of Cancer, and your South Node automatically falls into the 10ᵗʰ house, which has a Capricorn undertone. Add the description of the *sign* of your North Node to this *house* position to deepen your understanding of your Nodal axis:

With the North Node in the 4ᵗʰ house you'd be wise to focus on the 3 H's: home, heart and hearth. Your home now, and your home life in your family of origin, has a huge impact on you and there's gold there for you! How do you understand the story of your life? What is your personal mythology? Writing a short memoir of your life with an emphasis on feelings and home life might be eye-opening for you. You may have focused more easily on your goals and career earlier in this life, or in a former life, and you may have even achieved a good measure of fame and self-respect along the way. Now however, its time to take the emphasis off the doing and put it onto the "being." And, one could say, it's time to "make home" and review your life story in front of your own hearth!

For 4ᵗʰ house North Node people it will be important for you to show empathy and validate your own feelings and those of others, and to work for emotional security in this life. You would be wise to focus on the process of getting things done, rather than the ego satisfaction alone, of the job finished. When you focus on your self and not try to take charge without fully understanding the situation, you win. Use your intuition! You don't need to feel overly responsible anymore. You also don't need to hide feelings and fears in intimate relationships or always do what is socially acceptable rather than totally honest. By understanding and accepting other's fluctuating moods without judgment, you can find the "job" gets done anyway, and people are much happier when their feelings are honored.

The movement from the outer-world orientation of the tenth house, to the fourth house of one's inner world of family and personal mythology, suggests the wisdom of not sacrificing your personal life in the pursuit of worldly ambition. It hints of a need to focus more on the process of doing things rather than the goal or end result.

We also hear a suggestion implying that the personal subjective response to life is the right one for you—and that as Jungian analyst, Jim Hollis once said: "Reject the seductive impulse to encapsulate the *mystery* by reason." The 4th house and Cancer is ruled by the Moon, and you don't want to sacrifice the mystery and process of life to logic, reason, and anything that diminishes the depth of the inner response. Now you can afford to feel the mystery, rather than intellectually analyze it.

In former lives, or earlier in this life, you may have trained yourself to repress feelings, instincts, sensual enjoyment for the sake of what needed to be done. You may have achieved positions of authority or respect, but you may have been separated from a sweeter flow of family interactions and personal reflection. This life is now meant to create a better balance between accomplishing things and nourishing and supporting yourself and others.

As you turn on your path and retrieve the gold in the shadow of your South Node of Capricorn, you use your commonsense and savvy by being an effective person in the life. You have integrity and ambition. And because you intuitively know how to be successful in the world, having done that in former lives, you now have the freedom and challenge to soften into a personal response to life. You can draw on both your masculine assertiveness with your feminine receptivity. Maintaining the balance of these two energies is key for you.

You are bringing gifts with you into this life that make you a natural leader and person of authority; use these 'default patterns' of behaving to stretch into the realms of emotion, mystery, and deep connection to Self. Inner work is as valid, or more valid, than outer work in the world in this life, so keep that soulful connection to your spiritual, meaning-making Self. And in loving yourself for that, you will love and honor others for their efforts to do the same.

North Node in Fifth House

Is your North Node in the fifth house? Then it has an undertone of Leo, and your South Node automatically falls into the 11th house, which has a Aquarius undertone. Add the description of the **sign** of your North Node to this **house** position to deepen your understanding of your Nodal axis:

Your fifth house North Node here wants to have more fun, and to see life as a game worth playing. It can bring out your entrepreneurial and artistic side as well. This Nodal axis wants to get personal—to risk the love affair, to have a child, to express itself creatively. It doesn't need to get philosophical and talk about saving humanity—-how about just one child at a time? And maybe that child could just be your inner child that's been neglected for awhile.

In past lives you might have been living on the sidelines watching others interact. You could have done great things as a scientist, an eccentric genius, a humanitarian....one who gave selflessly. Now it's time to "give to the giver" and to feel the flow of love in and out of your heart. You've earned it.

With this South Node you'll want to move away from the lower expression of Aquarian qualities: being emotionally aloof and detached, avoiding confrontation and intimacy, and having a tendency to think you always need more knowledge before taking action. Instead, it's time to take more risks, to reach for center stage, and to develop one's self confidence—-even if it means allowing your childlike qualities to come out more, and for you to be more of a "character."

Are your "friends" the kind of people who support your goals, your values, and see you for who you really are? Or are they people who have "just happened to you" along the way? With the South Node in the 11th house, there's a chance that you need to move up an octave in choosing friends who support you and your dreams, and also a need to leave behind peer pressure in any of its forms. It's important for you to become clear on who you are and who you want to spend your time with—move away from the crowds or groups that simply fill your time, and find a few "heart-mates" instead of acquaintances, and look for the community or place where you really belong. Look around a bit, so that you can sit at the right "camp-fire."

Having the North Node in the fifth house suggests you put the focus of your life on letting your light shine through self-expressive ways of being in the world. What would that mean for you? More creativity? More joyful times with friends, lovers, or children? Daring to risk your heart in a love affair? The fifth house rules short term relationships too—and its been said that people with many planets here, or one of their Nodes, may have some important "unfinished business" with people they may only know for a relatively short time—this is where the idea of love relationships, rather than marriage or friendship comes into play. So for you, don't rule out the importance of the people you meet even for shorter periods of time—you don't need to have a "love affair" but consider your relationships with the ordinary people you see for short times. How do you relate to these people? The Leo undertone of this sign suggests that you bring a generous open heart into all these relationships.

North Node in Sixth House

Is your North Node in the 6th house? Then it has an undertone of Virgo, and your South Node automatically falls into the 12th house, which has a Pisces undertone. Add the description of the *sign* of your North Node to this *house* position to deepen your understanding of your Nodal axis:

With the North Node in the 6th house, you'll want to become effective at handling the daily details of life and honoring the idea that one's life itself is the greatest art! You'll do well if you skillfully educate yourself to give your gifts to the world, for you'll find that you are greatly appreciated when you act on your dreams and turn them into reality. To do this, you'll need to have a workable ego that can withstands the pressures of the marketplace and the valley, rather than the mystic view from the mountaintop.

In this life, you bring with you a compassionate and perhaps mystical understanding of life which needs to be grounded in the affairs of this world. Having the South Node in the Twelfth House of the subconscious, hints that you may have spent many lifetimes in dissolution of the ego—either through meditation and spiritual quests or drug/alcohol abuse, co-dependence, of confinement in convents, prisons, or asylums. You might also have felt exiled or ostracized (or you emigrated) away from your community, and in this life there's a desire to regain your identity, your sense of Self, and to manifest your vision in a concrete way here on Earth.

An important soul lesson for you in this life-time will be to come back into your body and to feel the joy of health and sensuality. There may be a karmic memory of pain or deprivation in the physical body, and a default tendency to want to escape from this world. For you, spirituality means coming back into your body. In former lives, or earlier in this one, you may have experienced something of the impermanence and pain of life, and now there is the question— will you flee from this world, or truly make it a better place for yourself and others? The good news is that if your intention is the latter, you may rather easily find yourself with the teachers, guidance and inspiration you truly crave. But first the commitment must be made.

So with this Nodal placement, you'll want to leave behind: feeling yourself to be a victim, escapism and addictive tendencies, withdrawal and feelings of inadequacy, oversensitivity and the avoidance of planning. The qualities for you to develop are: bringing order to chaos, creating routines, focusing on the here and now, being of service to others, taking risks in spite of fears, and choosing to value and analyze details.

With this Nodal axis there can be a desire for a person or mentor who you can trust and learn from—

it's good for you to search for this, or for a school or a "way" that can help you. There can be a healthy desire to learn new things and to be a disciple ("to discipline yourself") to whatever it is you love doing. And when you emerge into the "marketplace" of the world and share your skills and talents, you may find that you have become the mentor as well as becoming your own best "author-ity." You have now become the author of your own life, in the here and now, and what you feel may be a deep sense of gratitude and peace.

North Node in Seventh House

Is your North Node in the 7th house? Then it has an undertone of Libra, and your South Node automatically falls into the 1st house, which has an Aries undertone. Add the description of the *sign* of your North Node to this *house* position to deepen your understanding of your Nodal axis:

The North Node being in the Seventh House, ruled by Libra and the planet Venus, speaks to the desire for harmonious and right relationship with others. It softens the Arian independent Mars, and it asks a soul question of whether or not you will consider engaging with another person in a full respectful dialogue of "I and Thou." The North Node placement here in the house of partnerships and marriage, encourages you to seek out close one-on-one relationships, whether they are in friendships, in counseling relationships, in marriage, or in business. It also asks that you learn to accept the paradoxical nature of human relationships in which you are called to balance the opposite qualities of light and shadow, good and bad. Accepting the humanness in oneself and others, with compassionate understanding and forgiveness is a huge part of this placement.

Having a South Node in the first house reflects the pattern of the independent Aries-like hero/heroine, who is on a quest to know who they are and to move assertively into the world. Some people see the Aries archetype as the warrior—the spiritual warrior or the hero in the story that begins: "Once upon a time there was a......." By suggesting this hero/warrior myth, the life story moves from being played out as the martyr, the outsider or the lost one, to the empowered one, and the one who transformed the Self. Freedom may have been an issue too; as anyone knows who is in relationship, freedom and expectation are things one negotiates within a relationship once the honeymoon period has worn off.

So the emphasis shifts to the North Node in the 7th—the relationship arena which has at its core the evolutionary issues of trust and commitment. How does one learn to trust and how does one balance needs for freedom with intimacy? Boundary issues arise, and it's problematic. With the South Node in the first house, it was all about you—your personality, your way of seeing the world, the nuts and bolts and nuances of how you would describe yourself, and how others would describe you. With the South Node here it describes a pattern of self-containment and retreat that caused an attitude to arise that may have felt cynical or simply alone in the world.

When we look at the South Node houses it's about the nature of the unfinished business in a previous life, and reflects the habits and mind-set that was needed to be finished or improved upon. Otherwise we would not be taking an incarnation at all. So, we look here at perhaps an exaggerated sense of independence or freedom or even excessive fear or worry—something which kept the person with this placement away from committed interaction with another. There could have been shyness or concern for the needs of others, or even a sense that others were "enemies"—and it may have been true. Even though there may have been great courage and wonderful assertive action, the compensating challenge is now of bringing in significant "Others" and partners into your life to round out your story. That's the 7th house! There's a move here from independence to inter-dependence. From aloneness to togetherness and partnership, and that can be pretty sweet.

North Node in Eighth House

Is your North Node in the 8th house? Then it has an undertone of Scorpio, and your South Node automatically falls into the 2th house, which has a Taurus undertone. Add the description of the *sign* of your North Node to this *house* position to deepen your understanding of your Nodal axis:

The Eighth House, with the Scorpio association coming from its ruler Pluto, is all about the willingness to die and be reborn if necessary in order to live a life of integrity. Like the phoenix that rises from its own ashes, the realm of the 8th house is the edge of transformation—where people go bankrupt, inherit a million dollars, or have a near fatal disease or accident that forever changes them—-the kind of "wake up call" that gives life deep meaning. There's no false security or living in the world of denial for North Node Eighth House people!

With the North Node in the eighth house, the house of Scorpio, we are called to find the emotional bottom line in all we do. It calls us to move beyond comfort, security, and even the simpler pleasures of life to a deeper level of truth and reality. It asks us to look into the eyes of the bully to find the frightened unloved child there. It calls us to become an empowered person and to dare to risk closing one chapter of our lives and opening a new chapter. It calls us to reach for the understanding of another's point of view, other than our own, and the willingness to intimately and dynamically become related with that "Other."

Having the North Node in the 8th house, ruling gritty transformations and other people's values, is a high calling. It brings up issues around intimacy, money, power, and healing—the kind of healing that people call "occult" because of its hidden nature. More than any other sign or house placement, the 8th house and Scorpio can heal themselves and others, and have a gift there. It also asks that you come into this power and healing by understanding another person's values when they're different from your own. Here too is where we can truly know the meaning of loyalty and trust. A North Node in this Eighth house is quite a gift if we can bring the 2nd house qualities of stability and integrity into a new life that is ambitious, effective and deeply connected with others.

We know that the South Node represents what we've come into this life with—-the gifts, the wounds, the challenges. On the most basic level, the South Node is where we are comfortable, because we are familiar with the territory, and in the Second House we may have been very comfortable indeed. Taurus, Venus, and the Second House all love security, good food and drink, loyal friends, and the type of pragmatic philosophy that is rooted in a confident and sensual understanding of life. The second house calls us to "own" the self confidence and independent re-sources that can create a good life on this earth.

So this Nodal combination honors that, but speaks to the need to move away from some of the security and comforts of this 2nd house towards the willingness to risk one's present level of security for a more vital and courageous life.

North Node in Ninth House

And...is your North Node in the 9th house? Then it has an undertone of Sagittarius, and your South Node automatically falls into the 3rd house, which has a Gemini undertone. Add the description of the *sign* of your North Node to this *house* position to deepen your understanding of your Nodal axis:

The call of the Ninth House, which is ruled by Sagittarius, is a North Node call to expand outside the mental, physical and spiritual bonds of your community, your nation, and your old ways of seeing things. It's a call to enthusiastically bring more of the world into your private life, to break up old routines, and to find a true spiritual rudder for your Soul's journey through this life. A North Node house placement here is always colored by whatever sign the Node is in, but it still carries the message of adventure—-asking you to read, travel, and to dare to understand your life from the highest perspective—the mountaintop view rather than the view from the marketplace.

This North Node is also in the realm of the higher mind, and it wants to be nourished by contact with anything that inspires and stimulates you to find "meaning." Because it seeks to expand into seeing life as a "quest" overflowing with many questions, it is not only the house of meaning-making, but also the realm of spirituality, religion, law, and philosophy.

The 3rd and 9th houses resonate with all the curious parts of our nature that makes us ask "why" and then urges us to share what we've learned. So teaching, speaking, writing, and telling our story can deeply gratify us. With a North Node here in the 9th house we are called here to see life as a grand Quest, and then to tell the story of our journey—to communicate what we know and what we've learned. With our 3rd house "street smarts" we're naturally savvy, and want to know "what's happening." But when not used well, a South Node here can be flighty and fearful of going too far or too deep. As the third house relates to the sign of Gemini, we could say that any of the negative characteristics of Gemini would apply here—-especially the puer or puella complex, also known as the Peter Pan Syndrome; hinting that a part of us is reluctant to take on the role of growing up and expanding our world beyond the familiar.

The crucial piece for the North Node in the 9th house is that we're being called to **slow down**! We've got to have time to truly digest what we've experienced, and get down to the soul of things. Glibness, speed and superficiality are the default patterns of this Nodal combination, and those behaviors have robbed our Soul of a certain depth and resonance. Now its time to discover the core values that give us a rudder to our life, but moving from reaction to reflection. No more quick band aids and easy answers now—you're being called to the Graduate School of the Soul and you can't use the cliff notes anymore.

The South Node in the Third House also suggests unresolved karmic issues with brothers and sisters, and situations from our early childhood. Communication is the key word for this Nodal axis, and how interesting it is that it is with our brothers and sisters and oldest friends that we are often trapped in an unending conversation that goes on for a lifetime.... even when we're not speaking with them. Karmic issues with siblings are another mystery, like that with our parents—why did we choose them; or why did they choose us? Did we know them before? Did we come together now to learn and grow more? As always with this Nodal placement, thoughtful communication is the key.

North Node in Tenth House

Is your North Node in the 10th house? Then it has an undertone of Capricorn, and your South Node automatically falls into the 4th house, which has a Cancer undertone. Add the description of the *sign* of your North Node to this *house* position to deepen your understanding of your Nodal axis:

In this placement the Soul is moving from a process-oriented emotional enmeshment in the family and clan to a goal-oriented position of being out in the world. Moving towards our North Node in the Tenth House, and/or Capricorn, means we are called to follow a grounded plan of conscious action and discipline to achieve our goals. We are meant to move out into the world—to make our professional lives a priority. No longer will we be bound by our emotions or co-dependent relationships, but rather we are headed out of the deep Cancerian waters of our family of origin and into creating a place and name for ourselves in the world.

The South Node here can succumb to moodiness and a dependence on others when in its default pattern. Because the South Node represents where we've come from earlier in this life and perhaps in a former life, it hints at the unfinished business due to prioritizing family above everything else. In this life the relations with family may still be deep and tangled, but whether there are good relations now or not, the point is that you can no longer afford to be defined and engulfed by family.

People with this placement are often more loved than they realize. It's important for them to make it a point to find ways to lighten up and creatively express themselves, as well as making time to keep company with good friends. They may find themselves given work and opportunities to succeed in the world in surprising ways using talents that they didn't know they had. Perhaps the challenge here is to learn to honor the fluctuations and inspirations and 'moods' of the lunar Cancerian nature while taking purposeful steps to achieve goals in the outer world. And what would those be? It's locked inside the heart of the Capricorn/Cancer nature, and only they know the way to dream it out into reality....

North Node in the Eleventh House

Is your North Node in the 11th house? Then it has an undertone of Aquarius, and your South Node automatically falls into the 5th house, which has a Leo undertone. Add this to the description of the *sign* of your North Node to this *house* position to deepen your understanding of your Nodal axis:

With an 11th house North Node you need to ask yourself: Who and what do I really care about in this world, and how can I connect with others who have similar passions? Who is my community, my "tribe," my network of friends? Are they a default pattern of strangers or are they co-workers and friends? I often think of "networking" as an eleventh house good "idea."

The core of the healing process with an 11th house North Node is to learn to take in a longer, larger view of life, to think strategically, and to take time to make decisions and develop one's life. It takes time to learn to discern what is valuable and what is not, as well as what and who supports you. People with planets and Nodes in the 11th often don't come into their own till later in life....but they do blossom.

With the South Node in the Fifth House, the default pattern or the past life pattern of the Soul was concentrated on personal self-expression, risk-taking, and whatever brought joy and pleasure—-and some-times it was too much, too quick, and changed your life forever. Like joining the military for the wrong reasons at too early an age, or falling in love and get-ting pregnant as a teenager (and making a quick de-cision into parenthood)—all these can be tragic for some people. With this Nodal placement, the Soul has experienced some thing like this in the past—de-cisions that came too fast, too hard, and weren't right in the long run. Now there's a desire to learn discern-ment and to move away from any excesses and bad judgment calls from the personal ego.

On this axis we are called to work with other people in finding our true path in order to fulfill our hopes and dreams. We are not a solo agent anymore; we are meant to interact with others in those things that are most important to us. Personal risk taking now gives way to considering what is of greatest good to the whole—and consensus decision-making.

A fifth house South Node is related to the sign Leo, and when we read a South Node we read the negative aspect of whatever sign it rules. So here, we can see too much self-preoccupation, narcissism, combined with all the 5th house issues around chil-dren, love affairs, creativity and sometimes over the top hedonism. There's great creativity here—but in the past the energy flowed backwards and inward to the self rather than outward to benefit humanity. We are reminded here with this South Node that what we do slowly, strategically, and by careful planning, often works to our best advantage. And when we truly follow our hearts dreams, we find the groups of people who share similar dreams.

(A side note: The computer and all the new technologies are excellent 11th house tools, so finding "one's tribe" and networking with kindred spirits is made easier through using the internet. We no longer have the excuse of isolation due to physical restrictions, both geographically and personal. We have so many ways to find our 11th house soul-friends, and new ways to find where we belong in the world. Another 11th house group dynamic is embodied in all the 12 step groups—they are a great example of a healing and supportive group that has changed many lives.)

North Node in Twelfth House

Is your North Node in the 12th house? Then it has an undertone of Pisces, and your South Node automatically falls into the 6th[th] house, which has an Virgo undertone. Add the description of the *sign* of your North Node to this *house* position to deepen your understanding of your Nodal axis:

With a North Node in the 12th house we are deep in the "house that Carl Jung built." This is the area of the deep psyche, the unconscious, and with a North Node here we are wise to explore the body/mind/spirit connection in our life. How are they interconnected? It calls us to participate in all that lies beneath the surface levels of life, and to reach for what can be learned through the more subtle worlds of music, art, poetry, painting and depth psychology.

With a North Node here we are called to "the monastery" in the sense that it is a summons to explore all that is beyond the purely rational and to seek the spiritual call towards Self awareness. The 12th house has sometimes been called the house of troubles, because it can't be dealt with logically and pragmatically, and to do so doesn't benefit the person with a North Node in this house. However, the key to this house placement is that there is no longer any need for troubles, duties, obligations, humility and service! All those are embodied in the shadow of the opposite 6th house. As a 12th house North Node person you have earned the right to nourish yourself on the deep pleasures of the unconscious: gifts of magic, insight and deep peace.

The karmic pull of your past with the South Node in the 6th house will be one that tries to pull you back to be of help to others, with an emphasis on the skillful use of the mind and duty, rather than the promptings of the heart. The default tendency here is usually around thinking rather than feeling, working rather than playing, honoring logic more than intuition.

The North Node compensatory medicine here is a move away from the particular and detailed attention that the 6th house requires, to the spiritual "meaning-making" and boundary-less quality of the 12th house. This evolutionary pull towards the 12th house, which is ruled by Pisces, will be to balance and correct that tendency to dutiful work with a more imaginative and collectively conscious type of thinking. The yearning here is to create more compassion in our lives by simply loving ourselves and others more. We've earned a degree of rest and release from duty.

The high road for North Node 12th house folks is a fascinating journey into worlds where not everything is controlled, obvious, or as it appears to be. It's a world where even limitations, chosen or not chosen, can be a profound gift. Who has not enjoyed the occasional "mental health day" when we've stayed in our pajamas the whole day without leaving the house?

In the 12th house, the shadow and the gold that is buried in the unconscious longs for conscious understanding and acceptance. Jungian psychology and counseling, with its emphasis on creative expression of non-verbal feelings and images, and its encouragement towards unique individuality rather than collective moralities, can be very nurturing for 12th house people. However, it is worth noting that this placement is paradoxically, not an easy one, because it's not as consciously accessible by rational thought.

Chapter 15.
Going Deeper; Unraveling the Unconscious Story

"In all chaos there is a cosmos, in all disorder, a secret order." C.G. Jung

I can imagine advanced students of astrology going right to this section of the book first for some quick verification and to see if they agree with the finer points. However, going into more depth in examining the Nodes is not for everyone. You may have enough information to go on right now. But for those of you who want to explore the "plot" of the prior life story, you will find those connecting dots here. Because you may want to read just sections of this chapter, and because some points need to be referred to again, I hope you will forgive any overlapping and still find the answers to your questions here.

This chapter covers the issue of *squares to the Nodes* and the *Ruler of the Nodes*, the polarity of the Nodes, *reversed nodes in signs and houses, planets aspecting the Nodes, the karma and free will of the South Node, and two sections about what you don't want to know about yourself, and retrieving the gold in the shadow.* Whew! Sounds like it could be too much...and I think it could, that's why this chapter is not as long as it could be.

Other writers, such as Steven Forrest, delve into the details of these questions very thoroughly, however I have chosen not to go into too much detail here. I hope to give you just enough detail, but mostly I want to give you *the theory* of how to do it, and have you use your intuitive active imagination with it. My fear in giving too much of a "detailed cook-book answer" is that you may get a wrong "reading" of your self by overemphasizing some "details" and miss the more important point of synthesizing this information with the other themes of your birth chart, such as the basic brush strokes of Sun, Moon, Ascendant, and of course the notorious and ever popular, Pluto. I'm not saying the subtleties of the Nodes aren't important, I'm simply saying that if you use your "astrological imagination" with this, you are likely to come up with a truer intuitive "hit" on your situation than if I spell out how it might be.

That being said, we are still going to delve into the evolutionary theory here, while remembering that it is crucial to prioritize and synthesize all the elements in a chart. When we see what the North and South Node is doing, how do we see Pluto supporting this? What is Saturn summoning us to do? Are the

Sun and Moon and other planets in agreement or adding a paradoxical piece to this story?

Attempting to understand the basics of the Nodal story is an act of imagination, and it lends itself to error if taken too literally. We are looking for emotional truth, not literal facts. So when we look at what are the rulers and the aspects to the Nodes I think any extrapolations need to be "seconded" by the rest of the chart.

It's key to remind yourself too that when you are looking at planets aspecting the South Node you are looking into your prior life nature. Planets that are closely conjunct the South Node are like a planet conjunct the Sun, *except we are talking about in a prior life*. The bizarre thing here is that past life aspects and situations tend *to repeat themselves in this life* until we bring consciousness to these patterns, and accept or reject parts of them. It is uncanny how often the past life "parable" is really the current life story as well. Karma repeats.

1—Squares to the Nodes, the Planetary Ruler of the South Node, and Planets aspecting the Nodes—the big questions!

Squares to the Nodes are your karmic "Skipped Step." It is that extra piece of information, or that particular area of life which you tend to skip around, to deny, or to not engage with....so when you ask: How do I get to my North Node? How do I know how best to prioritize things? What has been left unresolved karmically from past lives? This is where we look.

Like using those cheating "cliff notes" to pass the exam in high school, you're now suddenly in need of knowing what you've skimmed by—you've got to turn around and go back—if your Nodes are squared, there's something you missed! The entire PLOT of your life story now may hinge on the overlooked skipped step you took along the way, and now you need to go back and do it the right way.

For example, say you have Saturn in Leo in the 5th house squaring your Nodes. There's a blockage suggested here—that's Saturn, constricting the joyful expression of your heart's generosity—that's Leo, in the 5th house ruling children, creativity, love affairs, and all things "5th house" related. You would then be called in this life to not avoid that skipped step, but to make more space for those things in your life now and to question what resistances you may have there. Have you dared to be creative? How much stage fright do you have? Do you engage in joyful activities with loved ones or children, and are you in touch with your inner child? Have you allowed the generous hearted nature of Leo to express itself in this life? The story of your *daring to do these things*, holds some of the "plot" of your life.

Not everyone will have a square to the Nodes. But for those who do it's an extra piece of insight. To understand it you need to let your imagination roam around the meaning of the planet that is squared. Again, what sign is it in? What house? There is something in the nature of this placement that is telling you what you need to do as part of your process of getting to the North Node. You need to pick up the unfinished business here—there is something about that sign and house placement that describes what that skipped step is! It may be as strong as a "complex" or as simple as a forgotten way of thinking that needs to be brought into your life now. You can understand that skipped step as being a karmic "bad habit" from a former life, or simply a blind spot in your psyche.

Blind spot? The skipped step is often what we don't want to look at or deal with—it's the missing piece of the puzzle, the dropped stitch, the piece that needs the most priority in your life now, and often receives the least. Bad habit? It may be as simple as holding onto an attitude of scarcity in this life. With that attitude, how can the gifted guitar player really do his best if he doesn't think he's worthy of spending money on a really good guitar? Sometimes what is skipped is just a tweak in one's attitude.

For example: today I did a reading for a woman who had so many skills and abilities, yet she was feeling quite stuck for a number of reasons. We touched on what those issues were about, but I was left with the feeling that if she would take care of her body/ health, then the rest would fall into place rather easily. She needed to address the square to her Nodes, which pointed to the 6th house of health. And, at this point in her life I felt there was a certain urgency to it, and with Jupiter there, it involved overdoing and issues with sugar.

❧❦

Jeffrey Green and Steven Forrest were the first I know of to call this aspect *the skipped step*. The blockages and distortions that are symbolized by the planet and house that is square to the Nodes is a critical piece to consider when looking at a chart. Yet nothing is ever truly skipped or lost—it's just put away till another time, or done unconsciously. But for those who want more direct answers to life direction and soul purpose questions, these aspects are a wealth of information. Ironically, as easy as they are to see, they're never easy to act upon.

‿∾⊱

The *astrological ruler of the South Node*—its ruling planet—is a very important lead to follow if you're trying to piece together the full past life parable or to understand the nuances of the Nodal quest. The ruler of the Node is the planet that rules the sign, and we look to where it is located in the birth chart and what aspects it makes.

For example: say that the South Node's sign is in Scorpio, with Pluto as Scorpio's ruler—so we look to what is happening to Pluto in this person's chart. What house is it in? What is aspecting it?

Can Pluto as the ruler of the South Node point to both the problem and the medicine to cure it? Indeed it can, especially if we look to the North Node. If the South Node Sign is Scorpio and its ruler is Pluto, therefore the Ruler of its *opposite* sign, is Venus in Taurus. The North Node. Perhaps you are being called to integrate Venusian beauty and love with the mysteries of the Underworld, or into the power dynamics of your relationships.

Another example: Let's say you have South Node in Sagittarius. It's ruled by Jupiter, and you see that Jupiter is in your 11th house conjunct Mars. So there's several pieces to put together here: the 11th house issues (groups, friends, and how they relate to your long term goals) are described or challenged by Jupiter, the self-confident archetype of expansion and abundance, and it's also conjunct the Mars assertive male energy. One could "read" into this configuration several ways depending on the understanding of the whole chart, but this information could be suggesting that you would be wise to pick up friendships with males (or strong females) who have something in common within a group—and that you bring into this group a "Jupiterian" attitude of self-confidence, meaning-making, and perhaps joviality. It also hints that you weren't able to do this easily in a former life, or earlier in this life.

What about planets aspecting the Nodes by conjunction, trine or opposition?

Essentially this is where you don't need a cookbook answer. Just treat it for what the planet and aspect means—ie if a planet is conjuncting, or opposing, or making a trine to your Nodes, think of it "classically" the same way as you would a planet doing that to your Sun. It simply is amplifying and describing more of what that Node is about—except that because you are looking at Nodal information, the important point is the aspects to the South Node hint of your past life patterns. You probably lived that planet out quite thoroughly in a former life.

A planet tightly aspecting your South Node describes you in a former life, and like looking through a piece of stained glass, it also colors your current life today. Read it for what it is! Moon conjunct the South Node? Put the puzzle together: Moon: mother, mothering, feelings, reactivity. What sign is it in? You have Moon in Sagittarius? Is Sag concerned with the balance of freedom and issues of communication? Is it expansive and over-bearing at times in its enthusiasm? Is this Moon/South Node in the house of close committed friendships and marriage, or is it in the house of career? Where then might you be acting out these South Node tendencies?

A planet conjunct the North Node is a piece of that North Node Medicine I've talked about before—

there's something about what *this planet embodies* that you need to bring into your life more. The energies of that planet may have opposed you earlier in this life, but now it operates as a compensatory function, and it is this way because the evolutionary theory postulates that you were *in opposition* to this planetary energy in a former life. It opposed you as a person, or a "the brick wall of reality" that you couldn't get around. Now you can use it, by integrating those energies into your life.

For example if you have Venus in Cancer conjuncting your North Node, you'll know that something about the nurturing nature of love in relationship is good for you now, and is what you didn't quite get right in a former life or earlier in this one. Then, you make note of which house it's in to tell another piece of the story.

This kind of Nodal expansiveness in a reading stretches the imagination to play out a few variations on a theme—why not? You never know what you might find.

Still confused? Let me say it the way Steven Forrest expressed it so well in his book, <u>Yesterday's Sky</u>:

*A planet opposing the south node hurt you or stalled you in the past. Read it negatively.

*That same planet, on the North Node, shows you the way forward. Read it positively.

Got it? =grin=

☙ ❧

2—Pluto and Polarities: the Yin/ Yang Symbol

Most of us die with unresolved issues. Most of us die with a few regrets and unanswered questions. We have held grief, and know of the illusions, betrayals, and expectations of ourselves and others that weren't met. Most astrologers look to the planet Pluto to tell more of the Soul-story about this aspect of life, as Pluto carries the archetype of the deep wound. When we feel our emotional body to be heavy with grief, when we feel anger, abuse or fear the potential of power and power struggles, then we know Pluto.

The South Node holds the history of Pluto through many unresolved past lives. So much of what we carry within us unconsciously is buried here. The personal unconscious, as well as the family unconscious, carries an "imprint" from these lives, as well as from our early childhood. Here are the blockages, the complexes, the issues of betrayal and lack of trust; here are the psychological distortions some of us call evil.

Perhaps it is within the archetype of Saturn that we are truly invited to do the work to find new endings to old stories, and to release and heal whatever is still undigested by the heart. Not an easy thing to do! The good news is that deep in our psyche is also a remembrance of inner truths, talents, and inclinations that only we can intuit. Some astrologers look to archetype of Jupiter for the story of this. Look to the sign and house position of Jupiter when you need to see more closely where you are graced.

But it is within the North and South Node that we hold the full duality of promise and pain. Just like the wound of Pluto, and grace and gift of Jupiter, each holds a part of the other within it. The symbol of the Yin/Yang with the circular dot in the center of each side, embodies the relationship of the Nodes what I call the "gold in the shadow." The curving symbol of the yin/yang with the complementary dots in each side, suggest the interconnection between the two.

We understand the Yin/Yang symbol as reflecting the intricate balance and connection between these two polarities: the progressive/light/ positive qualities and regressive/dark/ negative qualities. The Yin/Yang symbol shows the potential for the highest and lowest expression in each choice we make, just as each Node speaks to both what is unresolved and undigested within us, as well as being the "medicine" that will bring us greatest relief.

The North Node can be seen as where we are open to an "inflow" and where we *nourish* our Souls. However, there's something unfamiliar about the North Node, and like tasting a new food, we often don't know what to think about it. Do we really like it? Are we open to it? If we can take it in, it's our best cure; it's the vitamin that we're deficient in. We feed ourselves here.

In contrast, the South Node, in its highest expression, is where we can feed the world; it's our gift—it's something we innately understand and can give to others. The power of Pluto past and present, resides here. The South Node, in its lower expression, is like the tail of the dragon—it's where we release the bitter undigested parts—dare we say it's "where we shit." And, where we spread our un-healing pain into the world.

The polarities and paradoxes of the Nodes are not truly opposite—in fact, because every astrological opposition carries within it the seed of its opposite, like the yin-yang symbol, each side holds a piece of the other contained in it. So it's not all about just reaching for the highest expression of the North Node and struggling against the lower expression of the South Node—what is truly expressed in this symbol is the very human, imperfect movement between the two—a give and take: a dance.

When we are able to hold the balance, what "shows up" within us is an energetic re-engagement with life, an inspiration, and a *growing re-enchantment* with the process of our life. Ah...here is where we extend ourselves past our comfort zones—when we reach into that place where we can love more and truly give of ourselves. The surprise is that in the giving we are able to receive more, and because of the receiving, we are able to give more.

3—Reversed Nodes in Signs and Houses

How do you understand your Nodes when the direction they are pointing to by SIGN, is the opposite of the direction they're pointing to by HOUSE? Good question! The short answer is that the SIGN describes the kind of behavior and attitude that is optimal to use, and the HOUSE describes the particular area of life—of "where"—this behavior and attitude is going to find its greatest impact. And, it's important to realize that the Nodes are always on a polar axis with the signs and houses always opposite each other—so when they're reversed, it calls for a more subtle understanding of the dynamic. People and their charts are complex, and sometimes paradoxical!

I wrote a blog post on North Node Capricorn and here's someone who replied to having a reversal in their chart—he has the North Node in Capricorn but in the 4th house, Capricorn's opposite sign naturally, with the South Node in the 10th house, which normally rules its opposite sign—-as he says:

"This is all fine and good, but what happens when you have this placement with a North Node Capricorn!!!! It turns everything inside out. What do I do?" (He has the South Node in the 10th house, North Node in 4th house.)

So with a North Node Capricorn he is called to act on all the high Saturnian qualities of good integrity, and patient, step by step, goal oriented behavior.

He's called to move away from the "lower octave" description of his South Node in Cancer—-i.e. moving away from fluctuating, moody and fearful Cancerian qualities:("nobody cares to understand me and I think I'm running out of money.") It's a call to accessing the highest qualities of the SIGN—in this case, Capricorn—but in the realm of the 4th HOUSE of life: which is the family of origin, the way we see and frame the story of our life (our personal mythology), and all that has to do with the 3 H's: home, heart, and hearth. So somewhere in that area of his life, he's called upon to be a guiding person of integrity; the one who sets the goals and integrity of the home, who moves patiently to set realistic goals within the family for himself and others.....and the one who can frame his life story in terms of what was actually done, in spite of difficulties and outcome.

We know that following the description of the North Node sign is *good medicine*, and a great idea for all of us. When we succeed at "doing our North Node" it's the kind of thing we remember on our deathbed. In this case we have this confusion: the sign is descriptive of what we're talking about, and the house describes where in life the dynamic is likely to happen. Always we look to the SIGN first as being the most important thing to consider, and the HOUSE placement next, because the house system is the weak link in astrology. We may have our birth time inaccurate (which sets the houses) or we may use different house systems according to our astrological beliefs. So trust the SIGN first!

4—The Karma and Free Will of the South Node

Karma is about the law of cause and effect and reaping the consequences of what we have sown. It's also simply "habit" and all the default, comfortable, knee-jerk patterns in our lives. We can read about that karma in our South Node, for it is here that we see the blockages, the unresolved wounds and all the self-limiting ideas we hold. We see the description of that karma in the South Node as well as in the karmic placements of all the planets in our chart.

However, it can look confusing if we forget that all the signs and planets can be read both positively and negatively. They can all play out in our lives on a high octave or a low octave, and it's especially important to be aware of this polarity when trying to understand the karmic message of the North and South Node. We have free will to bring insight and consciousness to our reactive South Node patterns or not—

So in every karmic Node, and in fact, in every planet, there is a "story" there that reflects an ambivalence or polarity that exists within us. The Nodes in particular need to be understood as both problem and solution to problem...as the disease and the medicine to cure the disease! The South Node is a statement about your Soul's evolutionary situation either in a former life, or earlier in this one—and the North Node a formula or good suggestion for how to advance beyond it. Viva La Difference!

Here's a letter that expands on that, and brings in a curious situation:

Dear Elizabeth:

Your writings on the north nodes are the best I've found, thank you! My question is this:

My North Node is in Gemini, 4th house; South Node in Sag. in 10th house.

*My Midheaven (MC) is in Sag. 10th house.... so if my South Node represents things to move away from, but my MC is in the **same sign as my South Node**, which is my "career path," how do you recommend managing both?*

I feel torn—how can I consciously move away from South Node tendencies that are outworn, yet still play up my midheaven potential?

Thanks so much,

Karen

This question is important and similar to the questions: "If my Sun sign and South Node sign is in the same sign, or if my Sun is conjunct the South Node, how can I understand this?" The key here is to see the **difference between a high expression of a planet's energies and a lower reactive expression of the negative aspects of the sign.** In fact, all these situations underline the importance of making conscious efforts to reach for the highest expression of the sign. It doesn't matter if we bring in the midheaven (MC) or any other piece of information—it all still works the same way.

So, with Sagittarius for example, you want to keep the free spirited, optimistic, communicative ability of that sign, but you'll want to move away from its tendency to speak before it thinks (foot in mouth disease!), dogmatic thinking (disguised in a jovial manner), and a tendency to not seeing the multiplicity of Truth and different points of view. Sag loves to talk, teach, and travel; it needs to keep it's humility in the process as well. And as always, be aware of not overdoing with all Sag placements. Hope this helps clarify.

5—What You Don't Know About Yourself

Or maybe you disagree—you think you'd like to know everything about yourself—or perhaps you're curious to know what others sense about you and you don't? The Nodes in their polarity hold what the Jungian psychologists call the "inferior function" and the process of "compensation" is done through the integration of the Nodes.

What do I mean by this? Compensation, according to leading Jungian analyst Jim Hollis, is the most important principle that Jung identified. What it means is this: Whatever is true to consciousness is compensated by its opposite in the unconscious. So if you're acting "too good" or a bit too pious, you can bet that there's quite a bit of nastiness or violence lurking in the unconscious. What about those dreams you're having? What about the way your body feels? What about how unreasonably angry your sister makes you feel? When we try too hard to carry one particular attitude, such as goodness, ambition, courage, etc. you can bet that its opposite is being constellated in your unconscious. Or...and.....it then gets projected onto other people who annoy you by acting out those qualities you've dis-identified yourself from, and/or it goes deep into the body.

This is why we try to make conscious what is unconscious—why we try to not have our unconscious contents leaking out inappropriately in distorted ways at the worse times and places. This is why Jung said it is better to be whole than it is to "be good." When a person or a country tries to be too good, and doesn't integrate its own negativity and problems, it projects them out onto others—and then you get things like the ethnic cleansing of Germany from the non-Aryan Jews. Or you get the really nice woman next door who flips into a rage. A truer morality would be to look for the opposites in ourselves, in others, in our culture and then treat it with compassion. To not do this, drives those feelings and energies into the unconscious where they wait for a chance to express themselves—inappropriately.

This is what an understanding of the Nodes and our birth charts help us to do. Even though some astrological insights may be uncomfortable at first, if we would be open to exploring our personal "North Star" the North Node, we would find that it *ultimately* feels much better than our former patterns—-the South Node. The South is the area we've been mired in, stuck in the past, and failed at to some extent. The North Node is fresh—it's new territory. It's a call to try something new. When we consciously use these North Node qualities, we compensate for the undeveloped or wounded parts of our psyche and bring wholeness back into our lives.

However, as an astrologer and therapist, I find that most people simply don't "hear" what their

North Node is suggesting. It's in the realm of denial; it's the blind spot. We're all more likely to recognize the South Node because it's our default pattern. We know the South Nodes positive side—the gifts, and most of our sins and failings, even if we don't want to admit it. But when confronted with the new possibilities and challenges of the North Node sign and house and aspect patterns, there's usually a silence in the conversation. The information is trying to settle in, but it feels unfamiliar, and almost—-wrong. "No, that isn't me," I can almost hear a client saying.

The balance of the Nodes can be developed. The North Node holds the qualities, traits and areas of life that we are most unfamiliar with, and it's the particular arenas of life we try to avoid. "Must I really go *there*?" we ask. "Do I really need to be more *that* way?" We have an innate antipathy to this region of life. Yet if we want to be truly conscious and healthy, we would be wise to do as Carl Jung suggested: integrate the shadow—and dare to look at where we "compensate" both consciously, and unconsciously. When we look beneath the visible outward story of our life, we "attend to our Soul" and nourish ourselves deeply. I believe it's possible to heal what we didn't get earlier in this life, and create ourselves anew.

❧❦

6—The Near Death Experience: Retrieving the "Gold in the Shadow"

We retrieve the "gold in the shadow" of the South Node, of our past, when we've done the work of the North Node. Here's the theory: we grow up repeating the patterns of the South Node, and we use the "vehicle" of the astrological Sun to create an ego with which to live in the world—until the time of our first Saturn return at approximately the age of twenty nine. Somewhere in that "awakening Saturnian time" we truly begin reaching for those qualities embedded in the North Node, and in so doing, compensate for the excesses and woundedness of our past. We begin to come home to our Self.

When we've done this long enough to sustain a workable life—that is, when we've worked to use both the positive qualities of each Node so that we create a balance in our lives—it is then that we are ready to begin the process of retrieving the "gold in the shadow" of the South Node. It is then that we can safely approach what the Jungians call the *shadow* and extract something that is not simply a default pattern.

If we think of the Nodes as being like the yin/yang symbol we talked about earlier, we could visualize the gold to be the circular dot that is embedded within the space of each opposite. This astrological gold is a gift of grace that is available for all of us—and in my experience it tends to come around the time of the Uranus Opposition: somewhere between the ages of 38 and 41. It is at this point that the psyche intensely feels the anxiety and necessity for change—it must retrieve what it has not lived out to this time. And in so doing, people change. It is now that one sees people at this age doing all those things they've put off—moving cross country, divorcing, marrying, having a baby, leaving their job, finding their true vocation. They are now on a new journey.

The exciting thing about this is that we can now "take" and handle the goodness in our family karmic inheritance, and reap the rewards of latent talents. We can also take something from a past life experience that we've "earned" but perhaps not used skillfully in the past.

When I think of this, I remember the Near Death Experience I had around the age of twenty-one. After experiencing some of the classic luminosity of it, I also received a message—a message received through "automatic writing" saying that I would be wise to *ground* myself in the world in a very tangible way, and *not come back* to explore these "other worlds" until I had my feet firmly planted in this reality.

I took the message to heart, and became a potter for the first part of my life, married a Virgo, and had a child. It wasn't until my forties that I returned to school to get my graduate degree in counseling and became a full time astrological counselor and writer.

My North Node is in Taurus in the second house; my South Node in Scorpio in the eighth. I see this movement from South Node to North Node and back to the gold in the South Node with clients. The Nodes feel, not only like a directional pointer, but also like a tool of the psyche/Soul to create balance, and I believe we move between the two in ways that are both mysterious and yet somewhat calculable.

❧❧

Would you ponder one more thing before we end this chapter? Who doesn't ask occasionally: "Who am I beneath this story of my life?" Or, like in the myth of the Holy Grail, we may ask ourselves: "Who is it that I truly Serve?" The gods of family, finance, freedom and romance are always there, but there are others. For some the symbolic life of the Self/Soul is perhaps what matters most, for others that is a meaningless statement. Who is this Self that still holds a glimmer of numinosity, like a vague memory of a half-forgotten dream?

We've been asking in this book: What does it mean to quest for our soul purpose—to "attend to the Soul?" In Greek, the word "psychotherapy" actually means *attending to the Soul*. Somewhere in our life journey we may come to a "dark wood" and it is then that we are more *hungry for Spirit and thirsty for meaning* than ever before. Always the Self remains and asks questions of us.

And so we ask: who are we now? The Self, rather than the ego, wants to be attended to, and yes, psychotherapy might be a way to do that, but we also *attend to the Self* when we do anything that is in alignment with our true nature. When we feel something resonating within us and the timing is right, it's as if a harmonic chord is hit.

One could make a case that there are two kinds of soul work: outer and inner. The first soul work is in the fields and marketplaces, and in our streets and institutions. This is the work of the janitor at the local community college and the nursing assistant at the nursing home. Or perhaps it's the soul work of the single parent making dinner and doing homework with their only child at home. Within the routine and unglamorous work is the hard work that must be done, and here too, are all the barely noticed but special connections we make with each other—the kinds of connections that warm our hearts and touch our spirits.

The other kind of Soul Work is the reflective inner work we all do with ourselves and each other in moments of reflection, in therapy, and when we move into the symbolic and artistic realms—when we move into the language of the Soul.

In _North Node Astrology_ I've attempted to help you find what uniquely resonates with you, and to be aware of the timing of your life passages; your transits. Astrology can also help us see relationships clearer, as relationships are a critical part of our soul journey. It seems as if this Self has a deep yearning to be met by another "consciousness" in a space of freedom and possibility, and in this space to see *itself* more clearly. Perhaps that is a topic for another book.

We may have many names for this "Self" I've been speaking of...some may think of it as Atman/

Brahman; the connection between the God within and the God Out There. Others may see this Self as simply the unique individual they have grown into becoming. Others may call it Jesus. We know we are all seduced by diversions, distractions and ailments that pull us away from this "Self"—this part of who we are, and to not "put any other gods before Me."

My sense is that the call to reconnect with a guiding vision, or deep wellspring, grows more subtly intense as we age. We want to *rediscover* our life direction and soul purpose. Many of us look to find ways to live a deeper life more connected to Source, and reject easy answers and old solutions to this quest. Astrology and depth psychology, yoga and meditation may intrigue us. We may want to travel *down and in* now, rather than *wide and far*. Our imagination is re-ignited to new possibilities where we don't have to go farther than our living rooms...or the library or the internet. We take up playing the harp or reading Rumi or decide to learn Reiki. This desire to re-discover, re-connect, and replenish this wellspring always seems to rise again. This is the retrieving of the gold in the shadow. My hope is that this book has personally been helping you with this retrieving and replenishing.

7. Pulling It All Together Astrologically...A Question of Priorities

Two astrologers sat at dinner one night
And I between the two
Listened to catch a wise or wondrous word—
Like jewelers they talked
Each exclaiming the beauty of their gems
The profundity of their skills
The folly of the mind.
Their suspicious interplay
Left me hungry.
Two astrologers sat at dinner one night
And I between the two
Listened...
To their circumscribed landings,
Like bees...gathering no nectar."

That's not what we want! I wrote those lines many years ago when I was new to astrology, and it was sadly written the morning after what had hoped to be a night of inspiration. When you care enough to go deeper into astrology, and into understanding the North and South Nodes, it can get confusing indeed—but perhaps the worst thing, especially *to hear* as a client or friend, is when pride and astro-jargon obscure emotional truth.

But how do we even clarify things for ourselves? With so many things to consider, it's hard to know what is important and what isn't. As we all know, a little knowledge can be a dangerous thing, and we know we have to start at the basic understanding of the signs and houses, and work it up from there. So synthesizing the various elements and "pulling it all together" by prioritizing is a crucial part of the process.

We know we have to have a basic grasp of the chart as a whole, and the importance of the Sun as the evolving ego or vehicle of the Soul, and the Moon as the unconscious default mood of how the Soul feels—that's a beginning. The Nodes, being based on the Sun and Moon are next in importance, and intricately tied all together.

If we see the Nodes as *describing* the karmic journey, then the first step is to read the description—the SIGN of your North and South Node, and then to read about where this is happening in your life, what life arena is this getting played out in. This is the section of the chart, the HOUSE, that they each fall in. This tells you a lot, and is enough for many people.

If however, you want to delve deeper and begin to unravel the details in order to more fully understand your past life karmic inheritance, or "parable," you need to go farther. The next step to consider is what PLANET rules your South Node? What PLANET rules your North Node? And where is that planet located in your birth chart and what is it doing in terms of aspects and houses?

Following this trail begins a process that takes you from the deconstruction of the chart to a reconstruction of it—like working with a puzzle or mystery. You analyze the Nodes, and then you look at the *overlapping pieces of information* about them, and then let your intuitive mind play with those overlapping repeating themes. Let your intuition guide you at this point, and approach the subject now with heart and imagination—leave the astro-jargon behind at this point and feel your way into what might have been and what is now. And when you talk about it with someone else, remember that you are "treading on their life" and kind words and good ethics must accompany your story.

෧෯

Besides looking at the Ruling PLANETS of the Nodes, it is significant if you have a planet conjuncting the Nodes, that is, within about 8 degrees of either Node in your birth chart. If you have a planet conjuncting the South Node, then this planet describes something about *who you were* either in a former life or earlier in this life. For example: Do you have Mars next to your South Node? This Mars conjuncting the South Node brings an Aries survivor, pioneering, warrior, and entrepreneurial nature to who you once were. Any planet conjuncting a Node modifies the description of it.

Now if a planet is conjuncting the North Node instead of the South, then it describes two things—-one is that it's **good North Node Medicine** for you to integrate and embody those qualities described by that planet into your life now, and, it also suggests that in the past you were UP AGAINST someone or something that opposed you in a way described by that planet. You came up against a "brick wall of reality" that you had trouble getting around—and it had the quality of that planet. It may indeed have been a person, and in the case of Mars, it would have a lot to do with "showing up and having courage."

తోం తోం

The last part of prioritizing the Nodal story that is fascinating to look at revolves around the aspects to the Nodes. The aspects describe something more about the story or plot of your "past life parable." A square to the Nodes is a possible *skipped step*, as Steven Forrest describes it, and describes the unfinished business or skipped/ resisted/denied thing that we need to do (or be!) in order to reach our North Node potential.

This is what Evolutionary Astrology does—and the chapter on the skipped step discusses this. But don't be surprised if you don't "get it." It's truly like a meditation koan, and not something that we can easily see about our self. It's a bit of a blind spot, this skipped step from earlier in this life or a former life. You truly have to meditate on what the planet, sign and house placement is telling you, in order to get it. Keep all the possibilities open till you begin to see a pattern emerging from where there are overlaps or repetitions in the chart as well as in the puzzle of the skipped step. This is when another trusted person or astrologer would be useful for you—together you could ponder the ways you may have avoided or tried to live out this part of your life.

Chapter 16.
"You Can Make Astrology Prove Anything"

"You can *make* astrology prove anything," she said to me with a malicious little grin. "It's like the Bible—just pick the right verse and chapter, and you can make a case for God's approval or disapproval on almost anything—astrology included." My friend had been studying astrology just long enough to get both confused and excited, and I could feel the tense undertones of emotion mixed in with the pleasantries of our after dinner conversation. "Look at the choices," she went on, "mid-points, solar arcs, transits, fixed Stars, secondary progressions—just pick a time and you can back up anything you want to say with some aspect." She had a point there, but she was missing the larger picture of how astrologers work with the increasingly growing tool-box of choices we have at our disposal. And beyond that, she was missing something even harder to explain. But I wanted to try.

I understood her complaint about all the astrological systems: Vedic, Sidereal, Placidus, Koch....evolutionary, medieval, psychological.....can it really all be true and 'under one sky'? And if so, how are we to know what works best? And what should we expect from an astrologer when we have a "reading?"

As astrologers, we quickly learn that there is an almost overwhelming smorgasbord of choices to make, both in how "to do" the reading, and which techniques to use. I take a strong hint from the ancient alchemists. The alchemists understood the process of things—you take things apart, separate them, let them "cook," and then put them back together into a whole—a new synthesis. The Nodes are like the flask or cauldron that contains the heady mixture of astrological elements. In a reading you don't have time to truly let all the elements fully cook, but you, or the client can do that after the session....or in a particularly good session, you may get a strong "whiff" of the heady stew, and see the gold that is beginning to emerge.

As a counseling astrologer, I have a Master's degree in counseling psychology with an emphasis in the work of Carl Jung. Most of my astrology teachers used the tropical Placidus house system, and viewed the planets as mythological archetypes within the spiritual mandala of the birth chart. I believe in the same priorities that most of my teachers believed—that the nuts and bolts of a good astrology reading depend on:

a) a good understanding of the natal birth chart, b) the outer planet transits, and c) the inner planet progressions. I now feel that the North and South Nodes synthesize the message of the entire chart reading, so they are the *gold*.

Of course there has to be a solid understanding of the Sun sign, Moon sign, Rising sign and all the planets in the natal chart. The North Node and South Node, and the transits and progressions make a reading complete, and without them all I feel it's inaccurate. I think that *not* to include all of these in one session is wrong—separating the birth chart from the crucial transit "forecasting" feels like cheating—if the client is having a major life changing transit and the astrologer is only talking about the birth chart, how inaccurate is that! Or even the other way is wrong—to only look at the transits/progressions while not checking back to the birth chart can be hugely inaccurate.

For example, if the transits show a potential for being very accident prone at a certain time—say, some Mercury/Uranus/ Mars aspect is peaking, and the astrologer doesn't look to the birth chart to see if the person shows a vulnerability in their birth chart to being "accident prone," then it would be wrong to counsel them to avoid travel at that time. The astrologer could mention it, but not over-emphasize it, because the birth chart doesn't substantiate the claim. And the other techniques, such as solar returns, relocation charts, etc. are good too, but I only add them to the stew when necessary. Prioritizing is key.

Let's look for a moment at the basics. If you were to ask: Who am I?—-and then describe yourself in terms of your Sun sign, in most cases—not all—you would be recognizable by the traits of your "Sun sign." But people are paradoxical and complex, and a description of your obvious personality traits alone does not define you. And if your Sun sign is next to or conjunct another planet it changes the nature of the sign.

How do you perceive the world? What's your style? How were you seen as a child, and what's your persona or mask? This is your *rising sign, or ascendant*. It's also a hint of what you might look like—Virgo rising? You look younger than your age. Aries rising? Do you have something red in your appearance—a face mole or a red undercolor in your hair? Do you wear red a lot? The ascendant is about how we appear, and how we present ourselves.

The *Moon* gives us hints as to what makes you happy and sad. Do you love a challenge? Do you love to be a little feisty and dare to "feel the fear and do it anyway"? That could be an Aries Moon. Or would you describe yourself as being both introverted and extroverted? Are you happy cleaning out your closets one moment and then ready to dance by the light of the moon on the beach the next day? This could be a Cancer moon....especially if you were to tell me how much what your mother did and didn't do for you while growing up affected you. So, the Moon represents our emotional nature.

Each sign describes another part of us. We are complex creatures, and the astrological chart tries to describe so many things—-how we respond to authority and discipline (*Saturn*), how we are rebellious or not (*Uranus*), how we feel about spirituality, getting high and boundaries (*Neptune*), where we are lucky, expansive or gifted (*Jupiter*), and even how we experience and handle life's toughest moments (*Pluto*).

ॐ◌

The chart is a fascinating yet inexact map of the territory of our lives. The wild card is that we have free will to play out the signs and aspects. We can bring consciousness and energy to them, or we can play on our strengths and go for an easy ride. We inherit a family karmic inheritance that predisposes us to certain ways of behaving that are not as easy to change as our hair color. And at every moment of our lives we have an assortment of different challenges and moods—these "transits and progressions." A good astrologer should trace the pattern of particular challenges and opportunities and help you prepare for and accept the stage of life you're in at the moment.

So when you have an astrological reading done, the astrologer will tend to describe you in terms of all the different facets or signs, and then look at what is happening to you in the present moment by looking at the patterns of transits and progressions. However, there is always *the big picture*. And the big picture is the Nodes. Your karmic story.

∂◦◦∂

Here's another way to look at it: my bias is that the best "readings" are not the ones in which I rely heavily on technique and prediction but simply when the metaphors I use allow the client to see deeply into their life. I know this is happening when they start looking at the question *behind* the question that they presented initially. And when the particulars of the client's experience match strongly with the symbolic description of the transits and progressions and the Nodal story, then there's a feeling of rightness and resonance. And then the technique becomes secondary to the quality of the moment of insight.

In every astrology reading, I suspect that no matter what techniques are used, the hope is that there will be a synchronistic moment of "ah-hah" when there's been an accurate mirroring of that which is above, to that which is below. Isn't that what we long for—-when some piece of the client's truth and the astrologer's technique rise up to a little epiphany together! Ahh.... then there is that *felt moment of meaningfulness* that makes all considerations of proof of technique secondary.

And so I offer you the idea that the technique that brings this about is already embedded in most systems: the idea of silence and reflection. Perhaps that is our only safeguard in truth-seeking; not forcing a prediction, symbolism or bias on our client, but honoring instead the idea that we are acting as instruments of the Divine. We can present whatever combinations of symbolism we think will be most evocative, but then, let's allow them a moment to swallow, to digest, and to truly look at their chart. I believe they will take what they need when we make it simple, clear, and in a language they understand. And in that moment of *silence* we give a chance for the Spirit to enter; for what the Jungians call the *numinous* moment, when you or your client looks at the chart and see the "answers" projected there—-upon the clear sky of the heavens above and the gods within. ~

Chapter 17.
"Surrendering to the Gods:" Where Jungian Psychology and Astrology Meet

I'm just finishing writing this book, and I'm aware of how it's been much more work than I originally thought it would be. And so I've been wondering, why did I write this book? And then I remember—I love making connections—to people and ideas. And I crave the sense "of belonging to the world" and of making heartfelt and thoughtful connections with others—people who playfully and seriously like to entertain these ideas. Jungians and Astrologers. Writers and readers. You and Me. I like to bridge the gap.

I also sense that there's a gap between the two worlds I hold so dear to my heart: the Jungians and Astrologers. The Jungians often view popular predictive astrology with disdain, yet quietly study astrology and talk about it with their friends (or their astrologer.) They tend not to write about it in their professional journals.

The Astrologers hear the reserve in their attitude, but often don't know what the Jungians are really talking about! To those Astrologers who focus on pragmatic approaches, the *oohing and aahing* of the Jungians and their general quacking over the "obvious" may make them seem like odd ducks. And to what use? These Astrologers will help their clients, like coaches, find their jobs or careers, but forget that the word "vocation" has its roots in the ability "to listen" to our deep selves. How do we get to that place of deep listening to the Self?

First, there's very short term counseling vs. long term counseling. Astrologers can sit with someone *once*, for a couple of hours talking with them about "their map of the psyche" and the astrologer will translate the archetypal patterns in a way that the client says would have taken months with their more traditional therapists.

A Jungian will sit with someone, for hours over many *years* helping their client listen to the various inner voices in order to discover who they essentially are. They give time for the inner work and the "alchemical process" to truly evolve and they support the client in the process. A sense of safety and love develops. It's powerful!

Both astrologers and Jungians honor the complexity of the Self, and the variety of our inner personalities—call it what you will: voices, archetypes, planets. Both know that we need to understand the "gold" and the "shadow" parts of ourselves. We need to understand the unique gold of Jupiter and the North Node, and the shadowy wounding of Pluto and the South Node. We need to bring responsibility into our lives—Saturn, and yet dare to take our freedom—Uranus.

Different words, same ideas. Dreams or divination? Both Astrologers and Jungians would agree that we project ourselves out into life and yet swim in the deep wine-dark sea of the unconscious. There are reasons beneath reasons why we do what we do, and our outer choices and inner revelations echo each other. The outer pragmatic solutions of the coach or astrologer will reverberate with the inner "Jungian" nourishing and unfolding process of the Self, and it will reverberate with life in the outer world. Neither better—both needed.

ॐॐ

Carl Jung was a trickster, a shaman, and a scholar as well as a spiritual man. His psychology came out of his life; he broke some rules, he kept to some. As John Perry, a Jungian scholar and friend of Jung once said: "There was always a little something magical about the way Jung's mind worked. He said that he felt himself to be more shaman than psychiatrist." And Jung studied and practiced astrology and alchemy. He was a bridge maker.

৵৹

I do not aspire to be Jung. But I have "an inner Jung" within me that desires to make connections and bridge gaps. I want to keep encouraging all the ways we can "attend to our inner life". We come into this life bringing woundedness and a sense of wonder and possibility. It's a great thing if we can stay aware of both, and how they continue to play out in our lives. And so then we ask....can I accept my fate and live it out well? Can I work within the limits that I have, and yet stretch to be all I can be? Yes, I think yes....we can all do that. And make bridges...

৵৹

Jim Hollis, in *"Enterviews with Jungian Analysts"* says: "The greatest gifts of Jungian psychology are found in recovering for us a sense of participation in an ancient drama...and in a mindfulness regarding the profound sea of soul in which we swim at all times. When most modern psychologies serve **the ego fantasy of control,** Jungian psychology affirms a more sober appreciation of **the summons to surrender to**

the gods, to what wishes to live through us into this world."

I love that last phrase! It hints of a knowing that something is calling to come through us, and that we are able to discipline ourselves—we can be a disciple to that which is calling us, but that we are also summoned to surrender ourselves to that which we must do. Jung spoke about this as "doing gladly that which I must do."

Sometimes it's just putting one foot in front of the other. If you've had a stroke, that is a huge effort! If you are caring for a baby, that is a huge effort! So the summons and the calling may sound soulfully glamorous at times, but as Jim Hollis is also suggesting here "Jungian psychology affirms a more sober appreciation of the summons." For everyone and anyone who has worked long hours at a task, we can appreciate that soberness also has its high moments.

෪෧

At the heart of Jungian psychology is the concept of individuation; the *"story of our coming home to ourselves."* And, as we've seen, the astrology chart can be seen as a road map of the journey, giving us clear points of reference along the trajectory of the individuation process and the complexes we carry within and meet along the way.

A good understanding of the astrology chart reveals the nature of the complexes and how we are individually *wired*. I understand Jung to be saying that we are each wired to experience life in a particular way and some of this wiring is unique to us alone and some of it is common to the collective. Astrologers see the individual chart as the blueprint of that wiring. It doesn't tell you everything about your life, but the chart will tell you how you are "wired," for example, in how you perceive your mother, and something of how you perceive nurturing and mothering in your life.

Jungians look beyond the personal, to the collective unconscious in humanity and see it as a universal imprint in our psyche, existing like an underground aquifer which we dip into at various moments in our lives. We've seen how Astrologers chart these moments of psychic "dipping" by looking at the transiting chart that surrounds the birth chart.

಄಄

Jungian analyst, Medora Woods, from Minnesota, sums up what I've been attempting to say in this book when she wrote to me and said: "The Nodal approach helps me see, as I do a reading, how someone is in touch with their individuation path. If they are blocked, the blocking complex is usually connected to the Nodal axis or the Moon. And then, their transits and progressions tell me where their current challenges and opportunities might be as they work in the direction of their evolutionary potential."

I love this combination of Jungian and Astrological thought and practice! I also know how hard it is when we come up against our own blockages repeatedly, and when we see that people we love may not get unblocked in this lifetime. But what a gift it is to be able to delve into the Jungian and Astrological world views, and to use this knowledge to help ourselves and others. This final poem came out of that sense of gratitude:

Soul Work; A Prayer of Thanks
"Let us give thanks for the work we do—
let us pay homage to the gods, goddesses,
symbols, signs and synchronicities
that make their appearance as grace
when the choice is made 'to ask and then to receive.'
when "Whether called or not called, God is present."

Let us give thanks for the chance to be messengers—
to bring the good news that all is well,
and all manner of things are well—
that life has meaning
that there is a rhyme and reason,
a warp and woof, an inner and an outer,
an 'as above, so below'.
Let us give thanks for this knowledge that grows into wisdom

that honors life cycles as well as well as season's cycles-
that sees meaning, where others see despair
that sees patterns, where others see chaos
that sees hope and evolution, where others see
none.

Let us give thanks for this ancient soul language
that challenges us to find the words to translate
the subtle geometry of the Soul; a language
that sees little acts of change as large acts of courage—
that delights at seeing the shy smile of recognition
when the personal story meets the larger story
and is truly heard.

Let us give thanks for this work
that repeatedly shows us how wrong we ma be—
that what we see first, is not all there is—
that people are far richer, more complex
and nobler than we imagine
and that what we see as God or human flaw
is flawless in design.
for the gift is in the effort
in the practice of reaching to understand
all the unknowable mysteries
for which we are so truly grateful."

                          -elizabeth spring, August, 2006

ﻥﻕ

Further Thoughts...

ABOUT ME~

Elizabeth Spring, M.A., has a degree in counseling psychology with an emphasis in the work of Carl Jung. She began her astrological studies with Isabel Hickey in Boston in 1969, and has continued studying (and certification) with astrologers Steven Forrest, Alice Howell, Liz Greene, and Sharon Russell. She has done post-graduate work at Pacifica Institute in California, Salve Regina University, and Krotona Institute of Theosophy. She teaches periodically at the Boston Jung Institute, and has lectured at Brown University, RISD, and yoga centers around New England. Elizabeth has been a psychotherapist and practicing astrologer since 1992 and is a member of the astrological organizations, ISAR and NCGR. Many of her published articles can be read on her website: www.elizabethspring.com or web blog: http://North-NodeAstrology.com Elizabeth's full bio, lectures, and teaching can be found on her home website as well.

MY WORK:

I'm available for counseling sessions, with details on: www.elizabethspring.com. These sessions are arranged by phone or internet, and most are 60-90 minute phone conversations based on your astrological birth chart, and your current and future transits and progressions. Sometimes relationship comparison charts are used. Follow-up counseling/coaching sessions with less astrological emphasis are also offered.

ABOUT US:

Do you have comments, questions, or ideas to offer? Do you have suggestions for my next writing project? Would you like to link sites or have me as a guest writer for your blog, or speaker for your group? Would you like me to lead a workshop for your group? Contact me at: elizabethspring@aol.com

BOOK DISCUSSION:

This book will be used for an interactive discussion on my blog: http://NorthNodeAstrology. blogspot.com Come share your thoughts and ideas! Do you have friends, or a book group who might be interested? You might enjoy using this book to open up new areas of discussion and contemplation.

❧ ❧

"Following threads
of chosen words,
One crafts a book
as one crafts a life—
Following threads
of small acts of choice
and courage—
Raveling and unraveling
the particulars of a life
Following the story-line home.

Catching hold of a purple thread of sorrow—
a yellow line of joy—
I needle through the cloth,
buttoning together the places of the heart
that must be bound.
Knarlly and knotted;
piecing and stringing
this tapestry, by such fragile threads—
I hide the back-side from view—
'Such a beautiful piece' they say, 'Strung together
by such rich, colorful threads'.

Yet I know how I suffered the broken
threads—
The illusions, false engagements, subtle be-
trayals—
So much paradox and possibility;
At times, the fabric barely held.

For far too long—
I'd look at the torn places
And tried to sew
Through button-eyes—
Un-knotted—
They released themselves—
As I sought to make connections
That were not mine to make.

But now the needle moves rhythmically
through the holy quartet
of a single button—
I see how the parts relate—
How the singular threads
Need to be knotted and interwoven—
Buttoned with the belief
That there are meaningful patterns
In this life of sixty-one years...
The stitches are beginning to hold;
the torn places are mending.

Slowly and persistently
the heart still cries out—
And what needs to become attached,
Attaches—
And what needs to become detached,
Detaches—
And nothing gets thrown away...
As I've become a keeper of buttons."
-elizabeth spring

᷍᷍